SS NOMADIC

SS NOMADIC

TITANIC'S LITTLE SISTER

PHILIPPE DELAUNOY

The
History
Press

Cover illustrations: *Front*: *Nomadic* serving RMS *Olympic* in the 1920s. (Annie and Philippe Duval collection); *Rear*: *Nomadic* in February 2018. (Author's collection)

First published 2019

The History Press
The Mill, Brimscombe Port
Stroud, Gloucestershire, GL5 2QG
www.thehistorypress.co.uk

British Library Cataloguing in Publication Data.
A catalogue record for this book is available from the British Library.

ISBN 978 0 7509 8807 0

Typesetting and origination by The History Press
Printed in Turkey by Imak

CONTENTS

Drawing by Maurice Lucas. (Fonds Maurice Lucas, Archives Départementales de la Manche)

FOREWORD

In the early 1900s many harbours in the world became too small to accommodate the rapid growth in the size of passenger liners being built to ply the Atlantic Ocean. Such was the case of Cherbourg in France. Large ships calling here would lay at anchor off the port and have their passengers transferred to and from the shore by tenders. The tenders would also be used for transferring baggage and mail.

In 1910, the White Star Line set about building the RMS *Olympic* followed by sister ships *Titanic* and *Britannic*. They were designed to be the most luxurious ocean liners ever built. To serve and compliment the new ships in anchorage ports, White Star also constructed the tender *Nomadic*, which was fitted with elegant lounges for use by passengers travelling in first class.

In 1911, the *Nomadic* started her life in the port of Cherbourg and the following year transported passengers to the *Titanic* for her maiden voyage. Now, over 100 years later, this vessel is still with us and on public display in Belfast. This book travels through time recording her varied and chequered career and her careful and meticulous restoration. This story is told by historian Philippe Delaunoy who is to be congratulated for this important and unique contribution to maritime history.

Commodore R.W. Warwick OBE
President, British *Titanic* Society

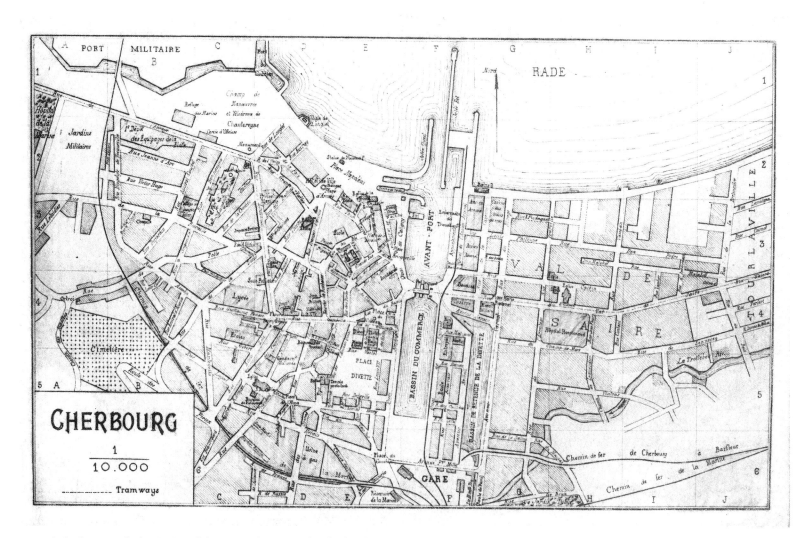

Map of Cherbourg at the beginning of the twentieth century. (Author's collection)

1

CHERBOURG HARBOUR

Over the centuries, Cherbourg has been both a port of call and a naval base disputed between France and the United Kingdom. In the seventeenth century, Louis XIV and his engineer, Vauban, were responsible for the development of Cherbourg as a strategic port on the Channel, initiating colossal maritime development works. This long-standing commercial port of minor importance, a city without university or cultural activities, quickly acquired a major role in the French homeland defence strategy and became one of 'the keys to the French kingdom'. Later, when visiting the city in 1811, Napoleon made Cherbourg a maritime prefecture and the Manche district capital.

From 1847, the geographical and technical properties of the port of Cherbourg attracted shipping companies linking European ports to the east coast of the United States and to the south coast of England. In 1858 a direct railway link between Cherbourg and Paris was created – efficiently completing the ports's connections with the most important cities in Europe.

At the end of the 1860s, ships of the Royal Mail Steam Packet Company and the Hamburg America Line stopped in Cherbourg before crossing the Atlantic. On 1 August 1878, a Weymouth–Cherbourg line was inaugurated by the Great Western Steamship Company.

The development of transatlantic traffic was extremely rapid. Between 1869 and 1897, the number of stopovers increased from forty-seven to 143 and the development was still going on:

	Stop-over	Passengers
1869	47	2,000
1897	143	5,770
1905	322	40,000
1900	378	30,313
1910	557	68,673

The second wave of emigration took place in Europe between 1900 and 1914, primarily of people moving westwards from Eastern Europe. Their reasons for emigrating were not solely economic but also political or religious. Whatever the motivation, the dream remained always the same – finding a better life!

At the beginning of the twentieth century, the habour of Cherbourg had mainly developed through its involvement in military arsenal and submarine construction activities. In 1900 the Chamber of Commerce decided to take part to the transatlantic passenger business and the construction of a maritime station started in 1904, when a wharf was installed on the southern part of the Quai de l'arsenal. At that time the building was merely a small wooden barrack acting as a ferry terminal. But the 'station' quickly turned out to be too small to accommodate passengers for the transatlantic traffic to and from Cherbourg in a decent manner. In 1907, the wharf was extended to 125m. Following this, a new brick station was built on the pier, unveiled in July

The arrival of a transatlantic train in 1908 and tender *Ariadne*. (Author's collection)

BRÉSIL — URUGUAY
ARGENTINE — NEW-YORK
Services maritimes réguliers et rapides
au départ de Cherbourg.

CROISIÈRES
L'ÉTÉ : en Norvège.
L'HIVER : en Méditerranée.

Agents Généraux :
Société Anonyme ROYAL MAIL STEAM PACKET
12, boulevard des Capucines, PARIS

Royal Mail advertising. (Author's collection)

1912. The new building was extended by two wooden barracks to accommodate all administrative and immigration offices. The buildings and houses facing the station were later acquired by the Cherbourg Chamber of Commerce and torn down to allow the installation of three additional railway tracks. One of the tracks would later be shortened to allow for the extension of the station's building. A marquee was also built, to protect travellers from bad weather.

Shipping companies quickly understood they could make a lot of money with the transportation of emigrants. In 1907, the White Star Line made Cherbourg, the largest artificial harbour in the world, a port of call. Six year later, Cherbourg had become a hub for six shipping lines: White Star, Cunard, the Royal Mail Steam Packet Co., Red Star, Canadian Pacific and Hamburg America. The development of maritime traffic was so huge that Cherbourg struggled to provide sufficient accommodation. Later in 1922, Cunard, White Star and Red Star Lines created an emigration centre capable of dealing with the mass of emigrants in Cherbourg, the Atlantic Hotel.

Cherbourg Harbour didn't become a deep-water port before 1933 and therefore shipping companies developed a fleet of small steamships called 'tenders' to ferry passengers and freight from the maritime station to the liners anchoring offshore. The first tenders, used at the end of the nineteenth century, were paddle steamers. When developing its activities in Cherbourg in 1907, the White Star Line bought the 1894-built steamer *Birkenhead* from the Birkenhead Corporation and renamed her *Gallic*. However, *Gallic* was a precarious and temporary solution, as the limits of her capacity and interior design quickly became apparent.

At the time the White Star Line was developing its own business in Cherbourg.

SS *Kronprinzessin Cecilie*
calling in Cherbourg in 1908.
(Author's collection)

Cherbourg harbour and maritime
station in 1904. (Author's collection)

The maritime station in 1908. (Author's collection)

The maritime station and transatlantic tenders in 1912. (Author's collection)

White Star Line postcard. (Author's collection)

American Line postcard. (Author's collection)

Norddeutscher Lloyd tender *Lloyd* departing with passengers in 1902. (Author's collection)

The Atlantic Hotel. (Author's collection)

White Star Line tender *Gallic* in 1908. (Author's collection)

SS *Gallic* in 1910. (Author's collection)

Olympic and *Titanic* under construction in the Harland & Wolff shipyards. (Author's collection)

2

SS NOMADIC, BUILT IN BELFAST

White Star Line's ambitious project to compete with Cunard Line's ocean greyhounds *Mauretania* and *Lusitania* was *Olympic*-class trio *Olympic*, *Titanic* and *Britannic*. They were designed to be the largest and the most luxurious passenger ships in the world, giving the shipping company an advantage in the transatlantic passenger market.

On 25 June 1910 White Star Line ordered two new tenders to be used at the Cherbourg stopover, the SS *Nomadic* and the SS *Traffic*, from Belfast shipyard Harland & Wolff. They wanted these vessels to create the right first impression, reflecting the luxury passengers would appreciate on board the brand new *Olympic*-class liners. *Nomadic* was designed to this brief by naval architect and Harland & Wolff managing director Thomas Andrews, as was her running mate SS *Traffic*.

SS *Nomadic* was designed as a first- and second-class tender. Her interior design was comparable with those of the *Olympic*-class liners. She was furnished with beautifully carved wooden panels, wood and wrought-iron vestibule entrance doors, porcelain ceiling roses, porcelain water fountains, a bar surmounted with a large mirror panel, and various luxurious patterns. Her design and arrangement made *Nomadic* a very comfortable vessel. Despite the fact that she was primarily designed for first- and second-class passengers, a small third-class saloon was constructed astern the vessel. As on any other ship of the period, *Nomadic*'s third-class saloon was isolated from the first- and the second-class areas for immigration control reasons. The first- and the second-class areas were separated by iron gates as well.

SS *Traffic* was a third-class tender, ferrying freight, mail and baggage. SS *Nomadic* and SS *Traffic* were not sister ships as their arrangements, design, propulsion were completely different. *Nomadic* was larger than *Traffic* at 71m long and 11.3m wide and with a gross tonnage of 1,260 tons. Her engine room was fitted with two compound reciprocation steam engines with a power of 550CV, which power two tri-bladed propellers. Two single-ended Scotch-type boilers provided steam at a pressure of 100psi. *Nomadic*'s average speed was 10–12 knots. Speed was not a major concern, as the tender only had to sail thirty minutes from the quay to the roadstead. *Nomadic* was designed to carry 1,000 passengers. SS *Traffic* was 56.7m long, 10.7m wide and her gross tonnage was 675 tons only. She was motorised by a single double-expansion steam engine fed by a single-ended boiler. Her average speed was 8–9 knots. Both tenders were equipped with Welin Quadrant davits and two lifeboats. Some seats situated on the flying deck bridge could be transformed into rafts and provide extra life support systems.

Nomadic's keel was laid down on 22 December 1910 (Yard No. 422) on slipway No. 1, alongside RMS *Olympic* and RMS *Titanic* slipways No. 2 and 3. *Nomadic* and *Traffic* shared No. 1 slipway with passenger ship SS *Patriotic* (Yard No. 424), ordered by the Belfast Steamship Company.

The construction of *Nomadic* took five months and the hull was launched on 25 April 1911. The tender was then moved to Hamilton dry-dock where the fitting-out was completed. She successfully completed her sea trials on 16 May 1911. The French crew, under

SS *Nomadic* under construction on slipway No. 1 in April 1911. (Robert John Welch (1859–1936) © National Museums NI and Harland & Wolff Collection, Ulster Folk & Transport Museum)

A port stern three-quarter profile of *Nomadic* afloat after launch on 25 April 1911. (Robert John Welch (1859–1936) © National Museums NI and Harland & Wolff Collection Ulster Folk & Transport Museum)

NOMADIC IN FIGURES

Dimensions

Length	67m (220ft)
Beam	11m (36ft)
Draught	2.4m (6.6ft)
Decks	five

Tonnage

Gross Register Tonnage (GRT)	1,260
Net Register Tonnage (NRT)	800
Displacement Tonnage	1,276

Power

Boilers	two single-sided Scotch marine boilers
Furnaces	four
Boiler diameter	3.36m (10ft)
Boiler length	3.38m (10ft)
Pressure	100psi (7kg/cm²)

Engine room

Engines	two double-expansion compound reciprocating steam engines
Cylinders diameters	343mm (1ft 1½in)–686mm (2ft 3in)
Power	550CV (542.3HP)
Dynamos	two

Propulsion

Propellers	two tri-bladed bronze propellers
Propellers dimension	1.93m (6ft 3in)
Speed	10–12 knots

(Source: Lloyd's Register)

the command of Captain Pierre Bouétard, arrived on 23 May and began to familiarise themselves with the ship. The tender was eventually delivered to the White Star Line on 27 May 1911.

Happily the construction of SS *Nomadic* and SS *Traffic* didn't suffer from any difficulties. However, *Nomadic*'s 1911 register mentions an accident suffered by French seaman François Kérambrun on 27 May. While *Nomadic* was still docked in the Abercorn Basin, the gangway disengaged from its attachment points as the sailor was boarding the ship. Sailor Kérambrun landed on the deck about 6m down. The fall caused him a rib fracture and he had to be confined to bed for some days. He was able to sail back to Cherbourg on board the ship.

On 31 May 1911, Harland & Wolff shipyard was in the heat of a very special day. Not only was the new RMS *Olympic* handed over to her owners, the White Star Line, but even more importantly the new largest ship in the world, RMS *Titanic*, was to be launched. And SS *Nomadic* had a special role to play, ferrying White Star Line guests on board the *Olympic*.

The size of the crowd that gathered to witness the launch of *Titanic* in Belfast shipyard is estimated at 100,000 people. Ninety journalists and representatives of the press also attended the launch.

At 12.13 p.m., the hydraulic launching triggers holding the ship in place were released, and *Titanic* began her descent of the 772ft-long slipway. *Titanic*'s hull took sixty-two seconds to travel the length of the slipway and into the water. Five tugs then towed the giant liner to deep water.

At 2.30 p.m., *Nomadic*'s crew cast off the moorings to join *Olympic*. On board were, amongst other special guests, Joseph Bruce Ismay, Managing Director of the White Star Line; JP Morgan; Lord Pirrie and some other top executives from both the Harland & Wolff shipyard and White Star Line.

White Star Line commodore E.J. Smith took the command of the *Olympic*, and she left Belfast for Liverpool at 4.30 p.m.. At the same time, SS *Nomadic*, commanded by Captain Bouétard, and SS *Traffic*, commanded by Captain Gaillard, headed to Cherbourg. They both had to be in Cherbourg in time for *Olympic*'s first stop on the Continent on 14 June 1911.

For her first voyage, *Nomadic*'s crew was composed of four officers, six seamen, seven stokers, one waiter and two apprentices:

CAPTAIN
Pierre François Bouétard
SECOND OFFICER
Joseph Ropers
CHIEF ENGINEER
Maurice Fillon
SECOND ENGINEER
Henri Thomas
SEAMEN
Georges Esnol, Séraphin Glajean, François Kerambrun,
Henri Duval, Gustave Durand, Pierre-Marie Caudal
STOKERS
Charles Constant (alias Dusseaux), Pierre Grouet, Herlé Le Corre,
Clément Rouspard, Jérôme Bréard, François Bignon, Alfred Marais
WAITER
Auguste Ade
APPRENTICES
Emile Doairé, Yves Marie André

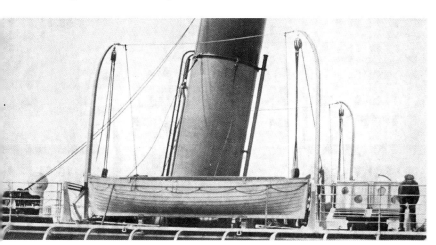

Nomadic's Lifeboat No. 2. (Welin Quadrant davits 1912 advertising calendar, Günter Bäbler collection)

White Star Line tenders *Traffic* and *Nomadic* in the Abercorn Basin in 1911. (Welin Quadrant davits 1912 advertising calendar, Günter Bäbler collection)

SS *Nomadic* passing *Titanic* after the former's launch on 31 May 1911. (Günter Bäbler collection)

3

NOMADIC IN CHERBOURG

Nomadic and *Traffic* arrived in Cherbourg on 3 June 1911 after a three-day journey across the Irish Sea and the Channel.

The press advertised frequently from April 1911 the construction of the two new White Star Line tenders and the fact that a French crew was to be recruited. Both vessels were described as 'miniature liners'. *Nomadic* was described as being of luxurious design and *Traffic*'s special escalator and winches for a rapid loading of the freight and passengers' baggage were noted.

The initial voyage crew were decommissioned on 6 June and a new team took over from 1 August 1911. Captain Bouétard remained on the bridge until he was replace by Captain Charles Patris on 1 September 1911. Second Officer Joseph Ropers, Chief Engineer Maurice Fillon and Second Engineer Henri Thomas remained on board. Some seamen and stokers were replaced so that the 1911–12 crew was composed of four officers, eight seamen, five stokers, one waiter and two apprentices:

CAPTAIN
Pierre François Bouétard (until 31 August 1911),
Charles Patris (from 1 September 1911)
SECOND OFFICER
Joseph Ropers
SECOND ENGINEER
Henri Thomas (until 9 September 1911),
Louis Marion (from 3 January 1912)

SEAMEN
Georges Esnol, Séraphin Glajean (until 5 June 1912),
François Kérambrun, Henri Duval, Pierre Marie Candal
(until 8 May 1912), Jean-Louis Cozic (until 15 July 1912),
François Longuemare, Gustave Durand (until 18 May 1912),
Paul Postel (until 2 January 1912), Louis Leledier
(from 9 May 1912), Edouard Corbin (from 9 June 1912)
WAITER
Auguste Ade
STOKERS
Lucien Delamer (until 29 August 1911), Alfred (alias Ernest),
Marais, Edouard Costa, Celestin Ade (until 06 September 1912),
Jules Leprince, Lucien Corre (from 22 September 1911)
APPRENTICES
Yves André (until 1 October 1911), Eugène Cozic
(until 15 July 1912), Robert Leven (from 5 June 1912),
Victor Béquet (from 22 July 1912)

When analysing the crew list, some names can be seen more than once. Being part of *Nomadic*'s crew was also a family matter.

Apprentice Eugène Cozic was the son of seaman Jean-Louis Cozic. Both were recruited in August 1911 and left in May 1912, going on to run their own fishery business in Brittany. *Nomadic*'s Register once again provides valuable information about Eugène, who suffered an accident on 28 May 1912. When boarding *Nomadic* on a pilot ladder, Eugène slid down one rung and was wounded in the right knee. Later, during the First World War, Eugène contracted a white growth on the same knee and his leg had to be amputated. He gave up his career at sea and became a shoemaker and a local councillor.

The name 'Ade' also appears twice in the crew list. Auguste and Celestin were brothers and spent some months together working on board *Nomadic*.

Despite the efforts of seamen strike leaders determined to hold up her departure, RMS *Olympic* left Southampton on 14 June 1911 early in the afternoon. The new 882ft-long superliner arrived in Cherbourg in the early evening and met Norddeutscher Lloyd liner *Kronprinzessin Cecilie*. This meeting allowed spectators to easily compare the liners' dimensions and led *Le Reveil* newspaper reporters to express their amazement, describing *Olympic* as 'a frightening mass'. Both tenders appeared tiny by comparison.

SS *Nomadic* ferried 450 passengers, boxes and crates from Parisian haute couture houses. SS *Traffic* was filled with baggage and mailbags. *Olympic* spent forty-five minutes in Cherbourg before sailing to the New World. It was hoped the White Star Liner would revisit Cherbourg quite often.

Their first mission was completed, *Nomadic* and *Traffic* began preparing to serve other White Star Liners; RMS *Adriatic*, *Majestic* and *Oceanic* were all expected to stop in Cherbourg over the following days.

Nomadic at sea in 1911. (Author's collection)

On board *Nomadic* in 1911. (Author's collection)

Nomadic departing with passengers in 1911. (Author's collection)

CAPTAIN PIERRE BOUËTARD

The names of the men who served in *Nomadic*'s successive crews remained uncertain until recent research led to the uncovering of the 1911–40 registration documents kept by the French Army Archives Department.

For years it has been suggested that Captain Boitard was commanding the tender *Nomadic* when RMS *Titanic* called in Cherbourg on 10 April 1912. It has now been certified that his correct name was Captain Pierre Bouétard, and the register proves that he was not in Cherbourg at that time.

Pierre Bouétard was born on 26 January 1869 in Pleudihen, near Saint-Malo. Pierre came from a family of Breton fishermen and he too took up this profession in 1885, when he was 16 years old. He graduated to captain in 1894 and commanded various tour boats in Saint-Malo between 1894 and 1907. He commanded the steamboats *La Bretagne* and *Jacques Cartier* successively. Ironically, the *Jacques Cartier* was later transformed into a guard vessel and based in Saint-Nazaire in the same squadron as *Nomadic* during the First World War.

Pierre Bouétard moved to Cherbourg in 1907. He commanded SS *Gallic*, the first White Star Line tender, from September 1907 to 22 May 1911. On 23 May, Captain Bouétard was sent to Belfast to take command of one of the two new tenders – SS *Nomadic*. He stayed at the helm until 6 June 1911 when *Nomadic* arrived in Cherbourg. He commanded SS *Gallic* again until the end of June 1911 and then *Nomadic* once more until 31 August 1911.

Pierre Bouétard move back to Saint-Malo in September 1911 and sailed as a skipper in various French ports until August 1912. He returned to Cherbourg in November 1912 and commanded first SS *Traffic* and then SS *Nomadic* until mid December 1914.

Pierre Bouétard died on 6 April 1915 in Saint-Malo, at the age of 46. He married Anne Marie Radenac in 1893; they had no childen.

Traffic and *Nomadic* moored at Cherbourg maritime station. (Author's collection)

Nomadic departing with passengers. (Author's collection)

Traffic and *Nomadic* returning to the docks. (Author's collection)

Clockwise from left: Charles Patris; Louis Leledier; Eugène Cozic; Auguste Ade; Gustave Durand; François Longuemare; Jean-Louis Cozic. (All from the Ade family collection)

EUGENE AND JEAN-LOUIS COZIC

Very little is known about Jean-Louis Cozic. He was born on 29 April 1868 in Pleumeur-Bodou, in Bretagne. He spent five years in the French Navy in Brest between 1884 and 1889 and obtained a certificate of good conduct.

During the First World War, Jean-Louis served as a seaman on the coal cargo *Sydney*. The cargo was sunk by U-boat 48 on 14 January 1917 off Cape Finisterre (Galicia, Spain). The men on board the *Sydney* tried to defend the ship against the submarine but ran out of ammunition and had to surrender. The Germans blew up the cargo after placing three bombs on board. They kept the captain and two seamen as prisoners and released the rest of the crew in a lifeboat. Jean-Louis and twenty-eight other men reached Cape Finisterre two days later.

Jean-Louis' son, Eugène, was born in Trébeurden, near Pleumeur-Bodou, on 30 September 1896. He became an apprentice in 1912 and SS *Nomadic* was his first posting. On 28 May 1912, Eugène was wounded on the right knee when boarding *Nomadic* on a pilot ladder. He spent some days at the hospital and then left Cherbourg.

Eugène was mobilised for war in October 1916 and was discharged for medical reasons one year later. Eugène's knee was infected by the Koch bacillus and he lost his leg. He received a medical discharge in 1919 and attended courses at the rehabilitation school for people disabled in the war. He qualified as a shoemaker in 1922 and returned to his birthplace to run his own business. Eugène Cozic later got involved in politics and became a local councillor. He died on 21 January 1971.

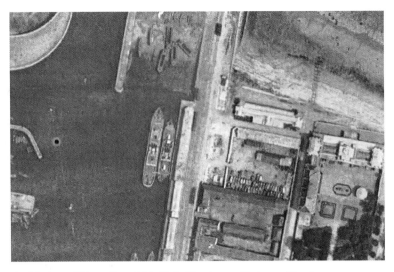

Aerial view of *Nomadic* and *Traffic* in Cherbourg Harbour. (Service d'Information Géographique de la Ville de Cherbourg)

Cherbourg maritime station, built in 1911–12. In the foreground is tender *Traffic* with some of her crew members. (Author's collection)

Battleship *Bouvet* and tender *Nomadic* in Cherbourg in 1911. (Bibliothèque Nationale de France, photographie de presse Agence Rol)

RMS *Olympic* entering Cherbourg waters. (Author's collection)

37. CHERBOURG — L'Embarquement des Voyageurs à bord du "Nomadic"

Nomadic loaded with passengers and bags in 1912. (Author's collection)

Clockwise from left: Eugène Cozic (front row, far right) at the Rehabilitation School in 1922. (Alain Cozic collection); Jean-Louis Cozic after his retirement. (Alain Cozic collection); Eugène Cozic before the First World War. (Alain Cozic collection)

4

TITANIC IN CHERBOURG

SS *Nomadic* really meets history on 10 April 1912 in the evening. The transatlantic train *New York Express* entered Cherbourg maritime station at 3.30 p.m. on that sunny spring day. A total of 172 first- and second-class passengers had undertaken the 6-hour journey from the Gare Saint-Lazarre in Paris to the Cherbourg docks.

Passengers were invited to enter the brand new maritime station (which was to be officially opened on 2 July 1912) and complete some administrative formalities. They were also informed that *Titanic* had encountered a delay due to a near collision as she was leaving Southampton. SS *New York*, tied to RMS *Oceanic*, had drifted off and almost hit the stern of RMS *Titanic*. She would thus reach Cherbourg one hour later than forecast.

At 5.00 p.m., 142 first-class and thirty second-class passengers were asked to board *Nomadic*. The remaining 102 steerage passengers took their places on board *Traffic*, which was already loaded with mail, baggage and some crates of French wine, Champagne and cheese from Normandy. 75,000lb of meat, 15,000 bottles of beer, 12,000 bottles of mineral water and 12,000 bottles of wine were brought on board as well.

Nomadic's waiter, Auguste Ade, was in charge of some of the richest people on the planet. *Titanic*'s millionaires boarded the first-class tender on their way back to the United States: industrialist Benjamin Guggenheim; New York millionaire tycoon John Jacob Astor and his wife Madeleine who was only 18 and pregnant; Sir and Lady Duff-Gordon; Denver socialite Margaret Tobin Brown; and Quigg Baxter and his Belgian fiancée Berthe Mayné, travelling under the pseudonym of Mrs de Villiers.

As they set sail at around 5.30 p.m. the tenders' steam whistles resonated in the Bassin du Commerce. SS *Nomadic* and SS *Traffic* headed to the Grande Rade. They stopped their engines thirty minutes later and waited another half hour for *Titanic* to enter Cherbourg waters.

At 6.00 p.m., Louis Castel, the French maritime pilot, was welcomed by Captain Smith on to *Titanic*'s bridge. The pilot guided the liner into Cherbourg Harbour. The White Star Line flagship dropped anchor in front of the dike's central fortress at 6.30 p.m., in the failing evening light. Unfortunately, many photographers skipped out on *Titanic*'s arrival in Cherbourg due to this poor light – they were expecting better conditions the next time the White Star Liner would call on the Continent – thus very few pictures of the occasion were taken.

Traffic was the first tender to board the liner. Not because she was closer to the *Titanic* but because she was carrying the first-class passengers' baggage. *Titanic*'s millionaires would therefore find their 'steamer trunks' already prepared in their cabin or suite, ready for a change of clothes. Then *Nomadic* reached the starboard side of *Titanic*, and her 172 passengers could finally experience the 'ship of dreams'!

The ballet of the tenders, passengers and freight lasted around ninety minutes. At 8 p.m., when it got dark, *Nomadic*'s whistle saluted the great liner and the tender headed back to the maritime station with some cross-Channel passengers on board.

Ten minutes later *Titanic* blew her whistle three times and weighed anchor. The majestic transatlantic liner turned around

Bassin du Commerce in 1912. (Author's collection)

The transatlantic train from Paris to Cherbourg in 1908. (Author's collection)

Cherbourg maritime station in 1912. (Author's collection)

and headed West to Queenstown (now called Cobh), Ireland where she would arrive the next morning.

For the *Titanic* passengers who boarded the liner at Southampton, the Cherbourg stopover was a rather anecdotal event, not only because it happened at sunset but also because most of them were having dinner when the small tenders were accomplishing their duties. Some passengers did recall *Titanic*'s stop in Cherbourg, however – like Thomas Andrews, who wrote to his wife on 10 April 1912:

We reached here [Cherbourg] in nice time and took on board quite a number of passengers. The two little tenders looked well, you will remember we built them about a year ago. We expect to arrive at Queenstown about 10.30 a.m. to-morrow. The weather is fine and everything shaping for a good voyage.'

First-class passenger Margaretha Emerentia Frölicher-Stehli wrote:

Warm greetings before the departure. We boarded a small vessel which will take us to the liner. The ferrying lasts thirty minutes. Greetings to the Reverend. I kiss you, Mum.'

The *Cherbourg Eclair* published the the tragic story of *Titanic*'s fate on the morning of 15 April. All public buildings flew their flags at half-mast. In Cherbourg habour, people could not help but think of the 274 passengers they had seen embarking in Cherbourg; 115 of them were lost.

On Saturday 19 April, *Olympic* was due to stop in Cherbourg. She had received Titanic's distress call when on her way to New York. Cherbourg citizens were shocked to see the characteristic silhouette of Titanic's sistership moored in the Grande Rade. To *Nomadic* and *Traffic*'s crew members she seemed almost like a ghost.

Nomadic departing with passengers. (Author's collection)

Some of *Nomadic*'s crew, photographed in May 1912. (Ade family collection)

5

NOMADIC AT WAR

When war broke out in August 1914, the White Star Line tenders *Nomadic* and *Traffic* were still being used for transatlantic liner service in Cherbourg. Transatlantic lines remained open until 1915 but closed after the loss of RMS *Lusitania*, sunk by German submarine U-20 on 7 May 1915. Later that year, RMS *Olympic* and RMS *Britannic* were requisitioned by the British government for war service. The maritime business in Cherbourg declined rapidly and the tenders remained nearly unused until their requisition by the French Navy in April 1917.

At that time, the Kaiserliche Marine had already developed the terrifying UC200 naval mine and a flotilla of UC-type minelayer Unterseeboote (U-boats) equipped with fourteen to eighteen mine tubes. The UC200 was a moored contact mine loaded with a 265lb TNT charge. Mines were anchored at predetermined depth and fired by contact with one of the projecting horns.

From the beginning of the war, it became vital to secure the supply chain from the UK and the USA to France. Bordeaux and Saint-Nazaire harbours were top priority targets for German minelayers and therefore French harbours needed to be cleared of this invisible and pernicious menace. The fight against marine mines had to be organised and the French Navy requisitioned thousands of trawlers, tenders, small boats and steamships of all sizes and converted them into auxiliary minesweepers.

The French Navy started to take an active interest in *SS Nomadic* and SS *Traffic* in November 1915 but they didn't order the preliminary study until March 1917. The French Navy shipyard in Cherbourg sent its report on both White Star Line tenders on 3 April 1917. The ships' general characteristics were studied and preliminary investigations for the installation of a sweeping apparatus were undertaken. The report, signed by Naval Engineer Raymond Daval, made it very clear:

… the transformation of both steamers *Traffic* and *Nomadic* would be fairly easy and doesn't require removing any roof, the sweep winch could be installed on the bridge deck after some minor reinforcement works and the kite wire would be sent directly from the winch to a 3 roller fairlead installed on the stern. Additional equipment will be required: a pair of davits each side for manoeuvring the floats, otters and depressors. That said, we must not ignore that the lack of power will reduce the average speed from 8 kts to 5 or 6 kts, both ships having poor performance in bad weather, and therefore they will be mediocre minesweepers. Only their shallow draft (1.85m for *Nomadic* and 1.53m for *Traffic*) makes them effective for sweeping activities.'

The requisition order for both ships came on 7 April, followed by various wireless messages urging their hasty transformation.

On 28 April 1917 Lieutenant Henri du Réau de la Gaignonnière was sent from Saint-Nazaire to Cherbourg to visit steamships *Nomadic* and *Traffic* and determine which transformations were needed for the crew accommodations on board.

Engineer Daval wrote a second report on 30 April, describing the necessary works:

German mine-laying U-boat UC5. (Library of Congress)

Sweeping apparatus: install a steam winch and its piping on both ships (to be provided by Maison Bossière in Le Havre), two pairs of davits and a three-roll fairlead on a raised platform.

…

90mm gun: installation aft on the shelter deck will not cause any problem. Ammunitions elevator needs to be arranged.

Crew accommodations: the third-class saloon will be fitted out as the crew quarters and equipped with tables, chairs and hammocks. Officers will be housed in the cabins on the Main deck. The first-class saloon aft on Main deck will be fitted out for the Captain's cabin. If needed, the wheelhouse will be covered.

Wireless: both ships are already equipped with two 12kw dynamos. One of them would be enough for providing lighting on board and the second one could be used for powering a wireless set.

Works began on 7 May 1917 and were due to be completed by the 27th. In May 1917 the Cherbourg Naval Base investigated the possiblity of installing of a captive balloon on board minesweepers *Nomadic* and *Traffic*. Engineer Richard Tremblot managed the project. He drew up the plan on 21 May. His report is still kept by the French Navy Archives Department:

Answer to wireless message 15810 dated 9 May 1917, here are the results of the study on the installation of a captive balloon on board tenders *Traffic* and *Nomadic*. As described on the plan the winch will be placed on the third deck after accomplishment of some minor consolidation and modification works. Some ventilators and railing have to be removed. Wireless installation doesn't need to be modified as the 60° clearance angle required the positioning cone doesn't cause any trouble.

…

The steam winch piping would be quite easy to install but if the boilers' operating pressure (7kg) is too low for the winch then we could use a 70hp Dion engine. An electric winch can't be used because of the low power dynamos (100 volts–100 amp each).

NAVAL ENGINEER RICHARD TREMBLOT

In May 1917, Naval Engineer Richard Tremblot worked on the installation of a captive balloon on board auxiliary minesweepers *Nomadic* and *Traffic*.

Richard Tremblot was born on 31 July 1889 in Paris and entered the Ecole Polytechnique in 1910. He graduated as a naval engineer in 1913. He was studying at the Naval Engineering School when the war broke out. He later requested an assignment to a field artillery unit and then joined the 33rd Artillery Division as an artillery observer officer.

He was recalled by the French Navy in May 1916. Followed some courses at the Naval Engineering School he was assigned to the French naval base in Cherbourg. First he was in charge of the Tellier seaplanes manufactory, and later he was assigned to the Technical Service for Maritime Aviation.

He married Marie-Thérèse Mauchauffée in February 1921 and became CEO of the Mauchauffée textile factory in Troyes. He retired in 1963.

Tremblot, who later took the nam Richard Tremblot de la Croix, lived a busy life. He was the president of the Chamber of Commerce of Troyes, president of the Aube Veteran Seamen Society, board member of the Reserve Officers Society, and gave a lot of time and energy as the president of the French Palsy Association. He was passionate about theatre, opera and music and gave conferences about the composer Offenbach.

Richard Tremblot and Marie-Thérèse had four children: Daniel, Philippe, Francine and Béatrice. Francine Aubin, born Francine Tremblot, became a renowned music composer and painter. She was the first female manager of the Paris Conservatoire.

Richard Tremblot. (Author's collection)

U-boat UC200. (Author's collection)

French auxiliary minesweepers in 1917. (Author's collection)

Minesweeper *Nomadic* entering Saint-Nazaire locks in 1918. (Department of the Navy, Naval History and Heritage Command Photographic Lot # S-586, Robert H. Helm's USS *Powhatan* (ID #3013) Photo Collection)

Captain Albert Levillain on *Nomadic*'s bridge – a drawing by René Pinard from *A bord des chalutiers dragueurs de mines*. (Paris, Devambez, 1919)

The west pier of Saint-Nazaire harbour in 1918. (Author's collection)

Despite the project being approved, the captive balloon was not installed until October 1917 when the ship had to be taken out of service for engine repairs. Later, the ship's weaponry was completed by the addition of Giraud-type anti-submarine grenades and smoke grenades.

Minesweepers *Nomadic* and *Traffic* were sent to Saint-Nazaire on 2 June 1917 under the command of Lieutenant du Reau de la Gaignonnière. *Nomadic* was the flagship of Saint-Nazaire's Minesweeper Squadron and commanded by the Head of the Basse Loire Minesweeping Group. The squadron consisted of escort ships *Crozon* and *Flandres II*, minesweepers *Nomadic*, *Traffic*, *Auroch* and *Kerdonis*, guard vessel *Jacques Quartier* and four sub-hunter speedboats.

During the war the French Navy used the Oropesa-type sweeping apparatus. The Oropesa is a streamlined towed body used in minesweeping. Its role is to keep the towed sweep at a determined depth and position from the ship. The device derives its name from the ship on which it was developed, HMS *Oropesa*.

At that time, no accurate mine detection device had been invented yet. The only way to destroy a moored mine was to tow a sweep from a small draft ship and cut the mooring wire. The released mine would then float to the surface and could be destroyed by gun or defused. It was an extremely dangerous duty, as shown by the list of losses – including the forty-eight auxiliary minesweepers sunk by mines or submarines between 1915 and 1918.

The sweep wires were kept underwater by a kite and wooden prisms maintaining a determined divergence between the cables. In order to avoid the whole sweep just sinking, it was connected on both sides to a float named the 'pig'. The cutting apparatus consisted of four cutters dispersed along each sweep wire. The mine's mooring wire would glide along the cables and be cut by one of the cutters.

Minesweeper *Nomadic*'s logs, kept by the French Army Archives Department in Cherbourg, document the missions undertaken by the ship between 1917 and 1919. The tactics used to clear the mouth of the Loire river from enemy mines consisted of making a number of successive passes through the North Channel (between Le Croisic and Pornichet) and the South Channel (between the plateau of Lambarde and the Pillar Island). It only took a few days for *Nomadic*'s crew to write their first mine on the scoreboard.

Seaman Dubocq – a drawing by René Pinard from *A bord des chalutiers dragueurs de mines*. (Paris, Devambez, 1919)

The French coast at Le Croisic, where minesweeper *Nomadic* operated between 1917 and 1919. (Author's collection)

An auxiliary patrol ship and Caquot type P captive balloon. (Author's collection)

Nomadic in Saint-Nazaire in 1918. (Author's collection)

An aerial view of Saint-Nazaire harbour in 1917 with an American convoy landing. Minesweeper *Nomadic* can be seen moored at the west pier. (Author's collection)

A cutter didn't work. *Nomadic* has a mine blocked in the sweep; a seaman will release it with a shear – a drawing by René Pinard from *A bord des chalutiers dragueurs de mines*. (Paris, Devambez, 1919)

Nomadic moored at West Pier (left side of the picture, behind the lighthouse) in 1918. (Author's collection)

an aeroplane
118 view of St. Nazaire water front showing locks, basins, and docks.

Aerial view of Saint-Nazaire harbour in 1918 with *Nomadic* moored at the west pier. (Author's collection)

The mine, cleared on 8 June 1917 at 9.00 a.m., came to the surface and was destroyed by escort ship *Flandres II*.

Based at Saint-Nazaire, *Nomadic* was also witness to the American Expeditionary Corps landing in France in June 1917. Lieutenant du Reau wrote the following in the Navigation Log:

26 June
4.00 a.m. – setting sail
5.30 a.m. – starting sweeping with the *Traffic*
Saw American convoy flown over by an airplane

28 June
7.30 a.m. – setting sail
8.30 a.m. – sweeping in the Main Channel
9.30 a.m. – saw an American convoy heading to St Nazaire harbour.

In its first thirty days of operations minesweeper *Nomadic* destroyed a total of nine German mines. One of them exploded close to the ship and caused damages to the ship's clock and the captain's washbasin.

Other damages were caused to the ship's hull on 25 July 1917 when she was manoeuvring near Saint-Nazaire piers. Bad weather and strong swirling currents made the ship difficult to steer. Despite her engines being fully reversed, *Nomadic* collided with the pier at 6.15 p.m. The damages caused to the ship's structure and to the sweep winch required important repairs and *Nomadic* was withdrawn from service for more than a month. In their turn, reciprocating engines were damaged in September 1917. During the reparations the captive balloon and its steam winch were installed on the Flying Deck Bridge.

The Caquot type P balloon was used for locating wrecked ships, floating mines, submarines. Later the ship was also equipped with a searchlight. The captive balloon was used many times from May 1918 to 1919, including to locate SS *Norhaug*'s wreck. The *Norhaug* was a 73m-long Norwegian coal cargo ship that had been sunk by a moored mine, laid on 23 May 1917 by UC21, a submarine based in Zeebrugge, Belgium, which sunk ninety-eight ships (134,063 tons) and damaged five others during the wartime period. *Norhaug* went down in fifteen minutes; five seamen asleep in the crew quarters were lost. *Nomadic* located the wreck in spring 1919 when the sweep wires hit the shipwreck. Later, the crew was luckier when discovering a wreck of another type – a large wine barrel!

LIEUTENANT HENRI DU RÉAU DE LA GAIGNONNIÈRE

Henri du Réau supervised the transformation works on *Nomadic* and *Traffic* in 1917 and their conversion into auxiliary minesweepers.

Henri du Réau was born in Poitiers on 2 April 1880 to a French noble family. He was the son of Henri du Réau de la Gaignonnière, landowner, and Marie Merland de la Maufreyre.

He entered the Naval Academy in 1898 and was put on the Training ship *Duguay Trouin*. He later served on dreadnoughts *Courbet* and *Formidable*, cruiser *Isly* and gunship *Zelée* from 1902 to 1906. Du Réau graduated as a French Marines officer in May 1907.

He then asked a military leave and worked as an engineer for the Sautter-Harlé & Cie. He specialised in turbines, electric equipment and electric generators. He joined the Navy Reserves in 1912.

When the First World War broke out he was assigned to the 2nd Marines Regiment in October 1914 and was wounded at the Battle of Brest (Belgium) just a few days after he joined the regiment. Just back from the hospital, Du Réau took command of the auxiliary minesweeper *Kerdonis*.

Du Réau was made lieutenant in April 1916 and commanded the Basse-Loire minesweeper squadron from 12 April 1917. He commanded *Nomadic* from April to December 1917.

He was then promoted to the function of Chief of the Waterway Police in Nantes until February 1919 at which date he was demobilised.

Du Réau later decided that he wished to take political office and became the Mayor of Cusy until the end of the Second World War.

He died on 27 January 1964 at the Barbelinière Castle.

Henri du Réau de la Gaignonnière. (Philippe du Réau de la Gaignonnière collection)

Nomadic in Brest in 1919. Note that the ship's name has been removed. (Author's collection)

Troopship *Leviathan* in 1919. (Author's collection)

On 18 December 1917 Lieutenant du Reau de la Gaignonnière was replaced by Lieutenant Albert Levillain.

On 8 March 1918, *Nomadic* provided assistance to the fishing boat *Angelus de la Turballe*. The boat was damaged after a mine exploded in its trawl. *Nomadic* towed the boat to a safer location near Pornic.

On 7 June 1918, *Nomadic* located a mine 40m from the escort ship *Crozon*. The crew first hauled the mine's anchor then the chain and the mine itself. The bomb was later defused on board the minesweeper. The commandant of Saint-Nazaire waterfront congratulated the brave crew and rewarded them with an extra ration of wine!

The French painter René Pinard and his friend Marc Elder visited the Saint-Nazaire naval base in December 1918. Marc Elder wrote a detailed report on a minesweeping campaign, while René Pinard painted some canvases on board minesweeper *Nomadic* and other escort vessels. The resulting collaborative work was published in 1919 under the name *A bord des chalutiers dragueurs de mines* (On board minesweeper trawlers) and contains twenty drawings describing life on board auxiliary ships during the war. *Nomadic* has been identified in four of the watercolours. In gratitude for the hospitality they received on board, René Pinard offered some drawings he made of Captain Levillain and a signed copy of the book along with an exclusive pencil drawing of minesweeper *Nomadic* with her captive balloon.

Nomadic and *Traffic* had succeeded in keeping Saint-Nazaire's waters cleaning; no more mines were to be found after 14 December 1918. When recovering their last trophy, Lieutenant Levillain, accompanied by seamen Lecarpentier and Tonnerre, encountered rough seas as he was manoeuvring one of *Nomadic*'s lifeboats. Albert Levillain was wounded when his leg was stuck underneath the boat, but luckily they all reached the ship safely.

Both tenders left Saint-Nazaire on 15 May 1919 and headed to Brest. They arrived on Saturday 17 May and the crew started to work decommissioning the ship. The White Star Line tenders were just about to sail back to Cherbourg when they were requested to spend some months in Brest, ferrying US troops on their way back to their homeland.

They were finally officially released in October 1919, having been sent back to Cherbourg in late August for major works to be undertaken before they could re-enter their service with White Star's passenger liners once more.

LIEUTENANT ALBERT LEVILLAIN

Albert Levillain was born on 4 May 1877 in Deauville. He joined the French Navy in Cherbourg as a volunteer aged 18.

A self-educated young man, he was passionate about engineering and he entered the School of Mechanics in 1896. Albert was promoted to a teaching role one year later in 1897, and later began his sea duties, joining dreadnought *Carnot*'s crew.

Levillain obtained the rank of petty officer in mechanics on 1 April 1900 and was allocated to the submarine base in Cherbourg until June 1902. He became an officer in July 1903 and he served again in the surface fleet as chief engineer on board the armoured cruisers *Admiral Aube* and *Lavoisier*.

He was detached to the Reserve Service in 1909 and travelled to Saigon (now Ho Chi Minh) where he occupied the position of harbourmaster until 1914 and founded the Indochina Flying Club.

On joining the military he requested to be assigned to a 'mechanical' unit, such as aviation, armoured vehicles or the navy. In August 1915 he joined the maritime aviation base at Dunkirk as an observation officer and took part on many heavy bombing raids on German submarine bases in Ostend and Zeebrugge. He later commanded the Dunkirk air defence force. From April to November 1917 he also set up and commanded the maritime aviation base at Perpignan.

On 9 November 1917 Lieutenant Levillain was assigned to the Minesweeper Squadron on the seafront of Saint-Nazaire. He stayed at the head of the squadron and commanded minesweeper *Nomadic* until March 1919. In 1918 Albert welcomed the French painter René Pinard on board *Nomadic*. Later, the artist offered him some drawings and paintings as a small remembrance of their friendship.

He was demobilised on 4 March 1919 and returned to Saigon. Albert Levillain commanded the commercial port of Saigon from 1922 until his retirement on 31 December 1935. He died in Marseille on 12 September 1946.

Distinctions and awards:
Madagascar Commemorative Medal 1894–95 (France).
Knight of the Dragon of Annam, 1909, and Officer of the Dragon of Annam, June 1926 (both France/Vietnam).
Croix de Guerre and Commendation for Bravery (France), September 1915: 'During an ordinary bombing mission on 7th September 1915, Albert Levillain – Observer – assisted an injured pilot in controlling and landing their airplane safely in our lines.'
Distinguished Service Cross (UK) in 1917.
Chevalier of the *Légion d'honneur* (France), 3 March 1919.
Knight of the Royal Order of Cambodia (France/Cambodia), December 1922.
Officer of the *Order du Mérite Maritime* (France), August 1931.
Officer of the Order of the Million Elephants and the White Parasol (Laos) July 1932.

US troops embarking SS *Leviathan* in Brest in 1919. (Author's collection)

Troop billet for SS *Leviathan*, 1919. (Author's collection)

US troops embarking on a liner in 1919. (Author's collection)

US troops boarding *Nomadic* in Brest in 1919. (Author's collection)

Nomadic ferrying US troops in 1919. (Author's collection)

Nomadic, *Traffic*, *Amackassin* and *Rintintin* tenders ferrying troops on 10 June 1919. (Author's collection)

US troops on board *Nomadic* and *Traffic* on 10 June 1919. (Author's collection)

Troopship USS *George Washington* in Brest. (Author's collection)

Traffic departing with US troops on their way back home in 1919. (Author's collection)

Nomadic ferrying US troops in 1919. (Author's collection)

6

BACK TO CHERBOURG

On 1 June 1919, Captain Jean Le Briand and Chief Engineer Maurice Fillon travelled to Brest to prepare for the return of *Nomadic* to Cherbourg. Maurice Fillon was the officer who knew the tender best, as he had served in this same role in May 1911 when *Nomadic* sailed from Belfast to Cherbourg. Chief Engineer Fillon had continued to serve on board until the war broke out. He was much appreciated for his technical skills and quickly developed a friendship with Jean Le Briand.

After two years of intensive minesweeping activities, *Nomadic* and *Traffic* arrived in Cherbourg in late August. When they docked at Cherbourg Harbour both tenders still showed traces of their military use. The railing at the front and aft the bridge deck had disappeared and the decking below the gun basements has been removed. SS *Traffic* was probably the more disfigured of the two tenders. They immediately underwent deep maintenance at Joseph Hamel shipyard. *Nomadic* was still dry-docked when White Star Liner *Adriatic* called in Cherbourg on 29 September 1919. Passengers were instead ferried by tenders SS *Seine* and SS *Traffic*.

Nomadic resumed service some weeks later and started her post-war career on 9 October 1919, ferrying passengers for the Cunard liners RMS *Caronia* and RMS *Mauretania*; the loss of many tenders during the war meant that the surviving vessels had to serve all of the shipping companies using Cherbourg as a port of call.

France's need for reconstruction following the war was colossal and as early as 1919 the idea of a new deepwater port was suggested. Tender captains, including Jean Le Briand, fiercely opposed the construction of the deepwater port. They claimed their resistance was due to security concerns; in fact they were mainly defending their own jobs, as a deep-water harbour meant the ships would be able to dock directly at the port and the fleet of tenders would then be useless.

By the end of 1919, the transatlantic traffic was picking up again, with an exponential increase in the number of stopovers and passengers. Liners *Adriatic*, *Mauretania*, *Caronia* and *Olympic* followed each other into the harbour. In May 1921, Cherbourg had six tenders at its service.

The 1920s experienced remarkable economic growth, based on productivity and speculation on the stock market. Science, cinema, fashion, arts and culture were vibrant and stars appeared in abundance – some of them travelling between the Old and the New Worlds on board transatlantic liners calling in Cherbourg and many being welcomed on board SS *Nomadic*.

Amongst the most famous names we find Marie Curie, who travelled twice on board *Nomadic* in May and June 1921 when she sailed to Washington to receive a gram of radium thanks to a campaign led by the American journalist Marie Mattingly Meloney; swimmer Johnny Weissmuller before he embraced a film career; actress Arlette Marchal; the 2.15m-tall giant Lehot; Denver's aristocrat Crawford Hill Jr; Russian playwright Constantin Stanislavsky; Queen Marie of Romania; and jockey Everett Haynes.

The redevelopment of transatlantic traffic continued and two more shipping companies selected Cherbourg as a port of call – the United States Line and the United American Line. In 1923, Cunard ordered two new tenders from Coaster Construction Co. Ltd in

42. – CHERBOURG. — La Gare Maritime et les Transbordeurs des Compagnies Transatlant

Tenders in the Bassin du Commerce, Cherbourg, in the 1920s. (Author's collection)

Montrose. SS *Alsatia* and SS *Lotharingia* were put into service in June 1923.

On 29 May 1925, eight steamers called at Cherbourg in the same day. Nearly 2,644 passengers were ferried by the tenders *Nomadic*, *Traffic*, *Alsatia*, *Welcome*, *Landemer*, *Lotharingia* and *Avenir*. Among them were 1,827 passengers travelling on board the liners *Majestic* and *Leviathan*. Although this day was exceptionally busy, the fact remains that the number of travellers passing through Cherbourg was subject to perpetual increase. From 1922 to 1925, the number of passengers increased from 112,744 to 184,597 and the number of stopovers from 644 to 877.

The increasing traffic in the 1920s was not perfectly trouble-free for the tenders, however. SS *Traffic* collided with coaster *Charmant* sometime in 1926, with White Star Liner *Homeric* on 5 June 1929 and with liner *Minnewaska* on 28 December 1929. Fortunately no serious damage was found.

The most impressive stopover happened on 18 December 1926 when five tenders and six express trains to Paris had to serve the 2,070 passengers landing from the White Star Liner *Majestic*. Tenders *Nomadic*, *Traffic*, *Alsatia*, *Lotharingia* and *Avenir* catered for all the travellers, 2,200 mail bags and 1,800 items of luggage!

In 1927, the White Star Line sold *Nomadic* and *Traffic* to the Compagnie Cherbourgeoise de Transbordement managed by a M. Hebert. Both tenders were still to serve White Star Line vessels, but also liners from other shipping companies. *Nomadic* and *Traffic* kept their White Star Line colours, but the crew and officers lost their jumpers and cap badges.

Captain Le Briand retired in December 1929 and was replaced on 19 December by Captain Elie Gauthier. Living in Granville. Jean Le Briand had commanded SS *Nomadic* for ten years. He was well liked and respected for his qualities as a sailor. Jean Le Briand and Maurice Fillon were commended several times for their exemplary maintenance of the ship.

Nomadic had a serious problem on 2 February 1932 when liners *Majestic*, *Hamburg* and *Orinoco* called at the same time in Cherbourg's roadstead. At 7 a.m. the liner *Hamburg*, coming from

New York, made a stopover. Conditions were satisfactory, but *Hamburg* was facing the wind, which was blowing furiously. Later the liner *Orinoco*, of the Hamburg Amerika Line, which came from the West Indies, arrived in port, and unloaded passengers, parcels and mail. Lastly, the liner *Majestic* passed through and was served by the tenders *Nomadic* and *Lotharingia*. At around 10 a.m. the two service ships returned to the maritime station. It was at this moment that the collision occurred.

Nomadic – with Mrs Edgar Wallace, widow of the English writer who died in Hollywood, and pilot A-E. Gadd, in charge of accompanying the passenger from Cherbourg to England via Le Havre, on board – was on her way to the harbour. At the moment when *Nomadic* was preparing to enter the harbour, she was hit by the steamer *Orinoco*, which had just weighed anchor. A violent shock was felt aboard the tender and some seamen rushed to the rescue belts. Though damaged at starboard aft, *Nomadic* was able reach the dock safely. *Orinoco*, on the other hand, had its bow severely damaged and witnesses could see water rushing into the hull at the waterline.

The next day, *Nomadic* entered the refit dock of J. Hamel shipyard, which set to work immediately. Fortunately the shock had occurred at one of the places where the tender's hull was the strongest, and it had largely withstood even this excessively violent collision. Nonetheless, the damages list shows distorted plating and twisted frames, the refurbishment of which required a lot of work!

On 1 June 1932, Auguste Roulet replaced Captain Elie Gauthier. Auguste Roulet commanded SS *Nomadic* for only a year. He was replaced by Leopold Rabecq on 30 May 1933. Both Elie Gauthier and Leopold Rabecq were born and lived in Regnéville-sur-Mer.

The Wall Street Crash of 1929 had brought the world economy into a deep depression – and transatlantic shipping was no exception. In this context, the United Kingdom could not maintain two competing shipping companies and the merger between the White Star Line and the Cunard Line inevitably occurred in 1934. In March 1934, the press announced the merger of the two companies, and the purchase of the tenders *Nomadic*, *Traffic*, *Alsatia* and *Lotharingia* by the Société Cherbourgeoise de Remorquage et de Sauvetage (Cherbourg Towage and Salvage Company), a subsidiary of the Le Havre towage company Les Abeilles.

Nomadic returning to the docks. (Author's collection)

These changes coincided with the start of a decline in transatlantic maritime traffic. To prevent or dispel some of the concerns that the changes might cause the crews, the company decided to keep the staffs and crews of *Lotharingia* and *Nomadic* in their posts, also assuring all crew that there would be no changes for those working on board *Alsatia* and *Traffic*.

Nomadic was renamed *Ingénieur Minard* by the Towage Company, in honour of Paul Minard, designer of the deepwater port, *Traffic* became *Ingénieur Reibell*, and *Alsatia* and *Lotharingia*

Nomadic serving Red Star Liner *Belgenland* in the 1920s. (Havet collection, Cherbourg)

became respectively *Ingénieur Cachin* and *Alexis de Tocqueville*. *Nomadic*'s and *Traffic*'s funnels were repainted black with a large red banner.

Commissioned late, the new Art Deco maritime station built by the architect Levasseur was inaugurated on 30 July 1933. French President Albert Lebrun made the trip in person especially for the occasion.

On 18 June 1934, a first docking by German liner *Bremen* took place at the Quai de France, followed by *Europa* in 1934 and *Queen Mary* on 27 May 1936 during her maiden voyage – an express call in Cherbourg for which she did not dock at the maritime station. As many captains feared, the new maritime station and the deepwater harbour put a brake on the use of tenders. Of eleven service ships used in the middle of the 1920s, only four were still in use by the mid 1930s.

Left: Captain Le Briand on *Nomadic*'s bridge. (Annie and Philippe Duval collection)

Right: Captain Le Briand on the bridge. (Annie and Philippe Duval collection)

Nomadic and *Titanic* 3D models by Mervyn Pritchard.

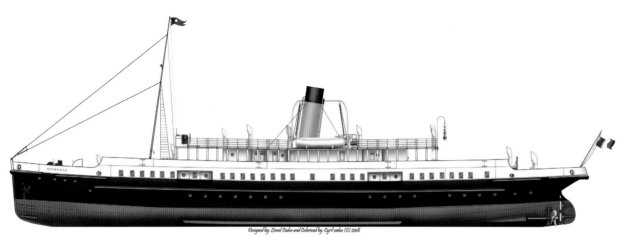

Nomadic profile by Cyril and Lionel Codus.

Designed by Lionel Codus and Colorized by Cyril codus (C) 2018

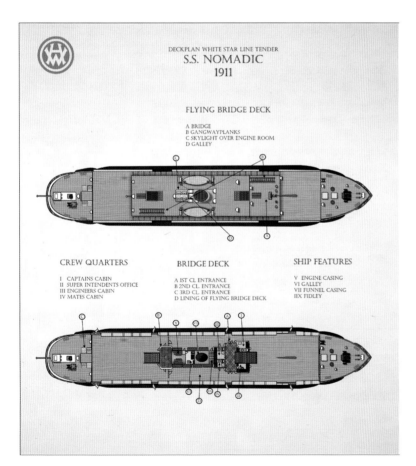

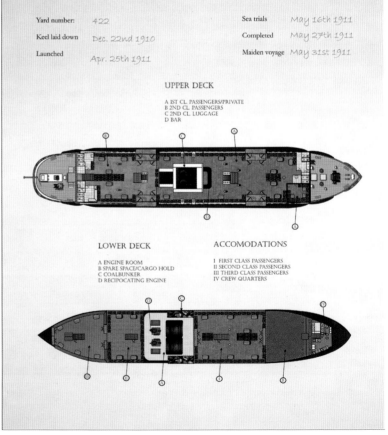

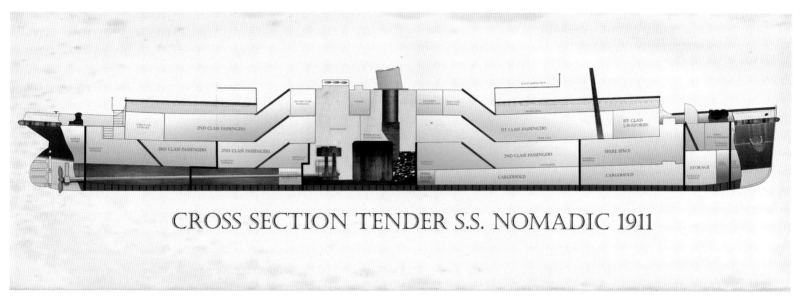

CROSS SECTION TENDER S.S. NOMADIC 1911

Nomadic in cross-section – a drawing by Jerry N.J. Vondeling.

Nomadic in profile – a drawing by Jerry N.J. Vondeling.

3D model of *Nomadic*
by Mervyn Pritchard.

Minesweeper *Nomadic* – a drawing by Jerry N.J. Vondeling.

A Float(s)
B Otter
C Cutters
D Depressor

E Sweep wire

Minesweeper *Nomadic* – a drawing by Jerry N.J. Vondeling.

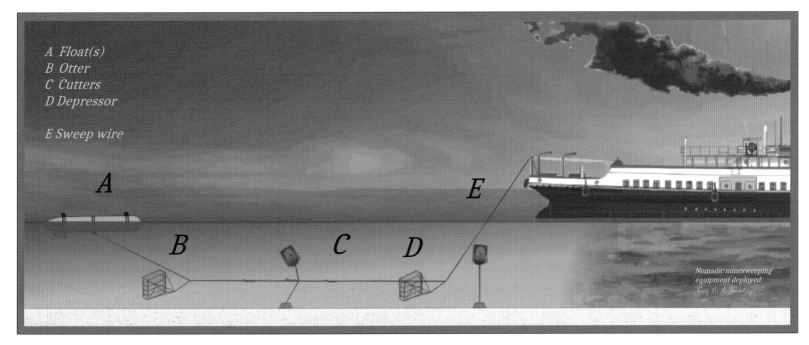

A Float(s)
B Otter
C Cutters
D Depressor

E Sweep wire

A

E

B   C   D

Nomadic minesweeping
equipment deployed

Minesweeper *Nomadic* and the Oropesa sweeping apparatus – a drawing by Jerry N.J. Vondeling.

'Firing on mines' postcard showing how mines were destroyed during the First World War. (Author's collection)

Clockwise from right: Captain Albert Levillain on *Nomadic*'s Flying Bridge Deck in 1918. (Drawing by René Pinard, Nomadic Preservation Society collection); Minesweeper *Nomadic* and her captive balloon in 1918. (Drawing by René Pinard, Nomadic Preservation Society collection); *Ingénieur Minard* in profile – a drawing by Jerry N.J. Vondeling.

Albert Levillain in a drawing gifted by René Pinard. (Bret family collection /Nomadic Preservation Society)

CAPTAIN JEAN LE BRIAND

Jean Le Briand was born on 22 February 1875 in Pleubian, Brittany. He started his career at sea when he was 15, in the areas of Treguier and Dunkirk. He graduated as a captain in the Merchant Navy in 1901 and served on board various coastal vessels near Saint-Brieux until 1906. He then moved to Cherbourg and received his first assignment as a captain on board the tender *Lloyd* on 1 April 1909. He commanded SS *Lloyd* for four years and then was transferred to the *Willkommen* of the Norddeutscher-Lloyd. In 1914, just before the war broke out, he commanded alternately tenders *Seine* and *Willkommen*.

During the First World War he joined the 10th Army Corps in Cherbourg as a Corporal. Jean Le Briand was promoted sergeant in January 1915 but was declared medically unfit to serve in the army some months later. He then commanded various coastal ships, again in the area of Fecamp and Saint-Malo. While commanding an armoured coastal sailboat, he had to defend his ship against a German submarine, and successfully sank the assailant.

When the war ended, Le Briand was recruited by the White Star Line and travelled to Brest with Chief Engineer Maurice Fillon in June 1919 to prepare SS *Nomadic* for her return to Cherbourg. Captain Le Briand and his crew brought *Nomadic* back to Cherbourg in late August that year. He commanded the famous tender until the end of 1929 and retired on 19 December of the same year. Jean Le Briand spent thirty-six years at sea, more than twenty-three years of these as a Captain.

Jean Le Briand was a highly respected sailor and, with Maurice Fillon, was frequently commended for his proper maintenance of the tender. In the 1920s, his crew, and that of the *Traffic*, frequently competed in the Cherbourg regattas. He also enjoyed competing in regattas for scale models.

Jean Le Briand was known for his strong character. One story tells how he grabbed by the collar and knocked over a representative of the Cherbourg Chamber of Commerce who had criticised the way he was maintaining the ship.

Jean Le Briand died in Cherbourg on 10 April 1936, twenty-four years exactly after *Nomadic* served RMS *Titanic*.

Jean Le Briand. (Annie and Philippe Duval collection)

Tender *Lloyd*, commanded by Jean Le Briand from 1909 to 1913. (Author's collection)

Jean Le Briand and Douglas Fairbanks on *Nomadic* in 1924. (Annie and Philippe Duval collection)

Captain Le Briand on the bridge. (Annie and Philippe Duval collection)

Nomadic serving RMS *Olympic* in the 1920s. (Annie and Philippe Duval collection)

Captain Jean Le Briand and Chief Engineer Maurice Fillon on *Nomadic* after 1927. (Annie and Philippe Duval collection)

SS *Leviathan* calling at Cherbourg on 13 March 1928. (Author's collection)

A car unloaded from SS *Traffic* in 1929. (Günter Bäbler collection)

Nomadic in the Bassin du Commerce in the 1930s. (Author's collection)

PAUL MINARD: A BRILLIANT INVENTOR

Paul Minard was one of the first people to fully understand the possible use of Cherbourg Harbour as a fantastic tool for commercial and economic development. His excellent engineering skills led him to anticipate necessary harbour improvements and the importance of the deepwater port.

Paul Charles Arthur Minard was born on 10 September 1858 in Pontgouin, near Chartres. As a young boy, he was a brilliant student. He entered the National Polytechnic Institute in 1878 and the French School of Civil Engineering two years later. Paul got his degree in 1883 and was assigned to the Maritime Works Directorate in Cherbourg.

At that time, the navigability and the security of Cherbourg's Grande Rade (roadstead) needed to be improved and Paul Minard joined the project in 1890 as a Deputy Director. By the end of the twentieth century the roadstead was protected by the western and eastern dikes.

Deeply committed to the strategic development of Cherbourg, the engineer strongly believed that the military vocation of the port was not incompatible with a civilian economic development. He observed the good relations between France and the United Kingdom since the fall of Napoleon, the positive view of the Admiralty on transatlantic traffic stopping in Cherbourg and the precedents for the use of military facilities for civilian purposes – for example, the French Navy's dry dock had been used by the Compagnie Générale Transatlantique for maintenance of its liner SS *Paris*.

Minard argued the need for a deep-water port and the absolute necessity of major harbour facilities to develop transatlantic maritime traffic. In 1914, he was assigned to the Department of the Navy in Paris and took the lead on the Deepwater Harbour Subcommittee. His case was helped by the fact that the First World War highlighted the need for deep-sea harbour facilities for cargo ships resupplying the front.

Left: Paul Minard wearing the Civil Engineering School uniform. (Radiguet family collection)

Below: Paul Minard, on the far left, and members of the French authorities await the arrival of the Danish sovereigns on 14 June 1907. (Author's collection)

3 VOYAGE PRÉSIDENTIEL A CHERBOURG
Les autorités attendant l'arrivée du Yacht Royal "Victoria-and-Albert"   Collection P. B., Cherbourg

After the war, Paul Minard met Camille Quoniam, future President of the Chamber of Trade and Commerce of Cherbourg. Both had long talks about the future of the harbour and began to build a strong case for their vision. They were convinced that liners being able to landing directly at the dock would greatly enhance Cherbourg's transatlantic traffic. Large ships would be able to dock at a 622m-long quay at any time, with no tide constraints.

The deepwater habour project was finally introduced in 1919 and agreed in 1921. It was such an upheaval that it was called 'the Mielle madness'. The construction started in 1923 and the very last facility, the giant Levasseur Maritime Station, was finally completed in 1933.

Paul Minard married Caroline Lepoittevin on 7 January 1884. They had three children and three grandchildren. Minard finished his career in Paris in 1923 as Chief Inspector for the National Directorate of Road and Bridges and was named a commander of the *Légion d'Honneur*. He died in Paris on 16 June 1941.

Right: Paul Minard, his wife Caroline and their son Pierre. (Radiguet family collection)

Below: Paul Minard visiting Cherbourg Maritime Station, and the tender that bears his name, with his grandchildren. (Radiguet family collection)

Clockwise from left: *Nomadic* ferrying passengers in the 1930s. (Author's collection); *Nomadic* and *Traffic* in the Bassin du Commerce. (Author's collection); Mr and Mrs Stillman, on their honeymoon, boarding *Nomadic* in 1927. (Author's collection)

Crew members preparing *Nomadic*. (Author's collection)

Nomadic, *Alsatia* and other tenders in the 1930s. (Author's collection)

Nomadic departing Cherbourg harbour in June 1930. Levasseur Maritime Station, under construction, can be seen. (Author's collection)

Nomadic seen from a liner's deck. (Author's collection)

White Star Line, Cunard and Norddeutscher Lloyd tenders. (Author's collection)

Nomadic under maintenance at Hamel shipyard. (Author's collection)

Hamburg Amerika liner *Orinoco*. (Author's collection)

Levasseur Maritime Station in 1933. (Author's collection)

Hamel shipyard, Cherbourg. (Author's collection)

Cherbourg harbour mechanical gangways built by Moisant-Laurent-Savey and MAN (*Popular Mechanics* magazine; Author's collection)

Clockwise from above: Advertising for the Société Cherbourgeoise de Remorquage et de Sauvetage; *Nomadic* testing mechanical gangways prior to their implementation; President Albert Lebrun unveiling the new maritime station on 30 July 1933. (All author's collection)

Ingénieur Minard docking at the Quai de France. (Author's collection)

Société Cherbourgeoise de Remorquage et de Sauvetage tugs and tenders. (Author's collection)

Ingénieur Reibell (ex *Traffic*) and *Ingénieur Cachin* (ex *Alsatia*) in Cherbourg Harbour. (Author's collection)

Ingénieur Minard serving the Canadian Pacific liner *Empress of Britain*. (Author's collection)

Ingénieur Minard and *Ingénieur Reibell* ready to ferry RMS *Queen Mary* passengers for her first voyage on 27 May 1936. (Author's collection)

Per R.M.S. "QUEEN MARY."

FIRST VOYAGE
SOUTHAMPTON—NEW YORK
27TH MAY, 1936.

Published and Despatched by:
FYFE & GREY,
THE STAMP SHOP,
UNION STREET,
BIRMINGHAM.
MADE AND PRINTED IN ENGLAND

SOUTHAMPTON
6 -AM
27 MAY
1936

Moncrieff P. Ford,
C/o Mr. Frank Wilson,
"STAMPS,"
100, Sixth Avenue,
NEW YORK,
U.S.A.

Queen Mary maiden voyage letter. (Author's collection)

Ingénieur Minard serving RMS *Queen Mary*. (Author's collection)

7

THE SECOND WORLD WAR

When war broke out between France and Germany in September 1939, tender *Ingénieur Reibell* (formerly *Traffic*) was requisitioned again by the French Navy and converted into a minelayer under the registration code X23. SS *Ingénieur Minard* (formerly *Nomadic*) stayed in civil hands.

In early June 1940, General Rommel's Panzers rampaged towards Cherbourg. The Cotentin peninsula resisted tenaciously thanks to French troops supported by the 51st Highland Division and the battleship *Courbet*, delaying the German invasion. This allowed 30,630 men of the 52nd British Infantry Division to leave Cherbourg and get back to England.

SS *Ingénieur Minard* tender took an active role in this evacuation, ferrying thousands of British soldiers and workers of the Amiot aviation factory to troopships lying at anchor off the port.

On 18 June, despite a heroic resistance, the Germans reached Carentan and Cherbourg capitulated on 19 June at 2.30 p.m. Submarines under construction in French Navy shipyards were destroyed and ships sunk in the port to hinder their use by the enemy, including X23. The German Navy later raised her and transformed the former *Titanic* tender into a coastal patrol ship. In 1941, the ship was eventually destroyed before the eyes of René Leledier, apprentice on *Ingénieur Minard* and grandson of Louis Leledier who had served on both White Star Line tenders. Her metals were then used for the German war effort. So ended RMS *Titanic*'s third-class tender.

During the evacuation of Cherbourg, Chief Engineer Marie took the command of SS *Ingénieur Minard* and escaped the Wehrmacht *in extremis*: Marcel Dubois, a stoker in the French Navy; Marcel Cussy, a cook; and many French sailors, boarded the tender and set sail for England. The ship crossed the Channel, despite the danger of being torpedoed or destroyed by a *Schnellboot* (German fast attack motorboat), and reached Southampton, where she was requisitioned by the Royal Navy on 3 July 1940.

Following the French armistice with Germany, signed on 22 June 1940, relations between France and Great Britain radically altered. Prime Minister Winston Churchill was determined that the French Fleet should not fall into the hands of the Germans and launched Operation Catapult on 3 July. This resulted in the Royal Navy attacking French battleships in Mers-el-Kébir, the requisition of all French vessels in British ports and the arrest of French sailors on British soil. Thousands of French soldiers, seamen and aviators were sent to military prison camps. In July 1940, the war between France and Germany was over and negotiations began between Great Britain and the French Government in Bordeaux for the repatriation of the soldiers held in the camps.

At the same moment, the Reich decided that the French ships in the English ports had a period of one month from the day of the armistice, until midnight on 22 July, to leave these ports and reach any French port. After this date, the instructions were given that 'all commercial vessels sailing under the French flag encountered at sea outside the Mediterranean will be treated as enemies by the German Naval Defence.' This declaration reached the French admiralty on 24 July.

Clockwise from left: X23 (ex-*Traffic*) in 1940. (Author's collection); Operation Ariel in Cherbourg, 15–17 June 1940. *Ingénieur Minard* helping the evacuation of the 52nd Division. (Imperial War Museum); The Bassin du Commerce after the capitulation of France, with X23 (ex-*Traffic*) moored at the 1912 maritime station. (Author's collection)

On Wednesday 24 July, 1,179 officers and sailors and 103 crewmen embarked on the liner *Meknes* for France, on the way back home to be demobilised. At 11 p.m., off Portland, the *Meknes* was sailing with all lights on and French tricolour flags painted on each side of the hull lit by large lamps. Despite showing her neutrality, the liner was pinned down by a German patrol boat and torpedoed. She sank in eight minutes, killing 420 men. Amongst the victims were Marcel Dubois, Marcel Cussy and former *Nomadic* crew member Ernest Leledier, who had also served on X23.

In August 1940, *Ingénieur Minard* was towed from Southampton to Portsmouth where she served as an Accommodation Ship for the Trawlers Base, like all requisitioned trawlers serving as Royal Navy Auxiliary ships. On 12 December 1940 the former *Titanic* tender was replaced by the decommissioned battleship HMS *Marshal Soult* and reduced to 'cleaning and maintenance'. She was reallocated for service as an accommodation ship from 1 September 1942 until the end of the war.

Surviving the Second World War, *Ingénieur Minard* returned to her owner in Cherbourg on 27 June 1945.

Compagnie Générale Transatlantique liner *Meknes*, which was torpedoed on 24 July 1940. (Author's collection)

Marcel Cussy, *Nomadic*'s cook, in June 1940. (Marcelle Leplanquet collection)

X23 (ex-*Traffic*) in 1941, just before she was scrapped by the German Army. (Author's collection)

CHAPTER 8

AFTER THE WAR

Back in Cherbourg in the summer of 1945, *Ingénieur Minard* resumed service after undergoing a significant amount of general maintenance. After several years of inactivity, the tender's machinery understandably needed a general overhaul.

The fleet of tenders owned by the Société Cherbourgoise de Remorquage et de Sauvetage quickly regained their importance in the transatlantic traffic service. RMS *Queen Elizabeth* was the first liner to return to Cherbourg, in 1948; at this time the reconstruction of the ferry terminal was in full swing.

After seven years of intensive work, the maritime station was reopened on 22 May 1952 by French President Antoine Pinay, just a few days after the great return to Cherbourg of RMS *Queen Mary*, which had not docked there since August 1939.

Since the Cunard White Star Line decided to return to Cherbourg, the maritime station regained its pre-war splendour, and many passengers and celebrities once again walked its halls. Rita Hayworth, Orson Welles, Charlie Chaplin, Liz Taylor, Richard Burton, US President Eisenhower, boxer Marcel Cerdan, French actor Fernandel, artist Salvador Dali and Belgian singer Jacques Brel were some amongst many to board one of the superliners.

By 1950, the level of pre-war traffic – around 80,000 passengers – was once more reached. Until that moment, technical evolution had especially favoured the maritime transport of goods and passengers. Transatlantic liners were the first ships to nourish the race for gigantism: journeys were faster and less expensive. On the other hand, the railway service between Paris and Cherbourg was as slow in 1968 as in 1929 and the hotel equipment was not significantly improved until 1963 with the opening of the 'Sofitel'.

The decline happened in two successive phases.

In the 1950s, the level of traffic fell to an average of 50,000 travellers per year, and remained stable until 1963. This was the direct consequence of the technological evolution of aviation following the Second World War. The construction of large four-engine bombers demonstrated the acquisition by the aeronautics industry of a remarkable technical expertise. Derived from these aircrafts, long-range civilian airplanes entered into service over the Atlantic. Only a small part of the clientele remained loyal to transatlantic liners, now victims of competition.

The second phase of the decline corresponds to the further explosion of air transport in the 1960s and the proliferation of large four-engine jets like the Boeing 707 and the Douglas DC 8 on transatlantic routes. In these difficult times for international maritime traffic and specifically for Cherbourg, tender *Ingénieur Minard* was commanded by Captain André Le Roi, a good friend of the family of Léopold Rabecq, who commanded *Ingénieur Minard* from 1929 to 1948.

Ingénieur Minard at the Quai de France in 1948. (Author's collection)

Ingénieur Minard serving RMS *Queen Mary*. (Drawing by Andrei Louis Alejandro)

Ingénieur Minard in the Bassin du Commerce in the 1950s. (Author's collection)

Ingénieur Minard in 1964. (Author's collection)

CAPTAIN ANDRÉ LE ROI

André Le Roi was born on 16 July 1907 in Regnéville-sur-Mer. As a young boy he studied in Coutances and Cherbourg. He graduated Officer Cadet at the Merchant Navy Academy in 1926 and became International Seafarer when aged 19. He was promoted to captain on 29 July 1932.

In 1925, while a student at the Merchant Navy Academy, André Le Roi served as a seaman on board Cunard Line tender *Lotharingia* and Norddeutscher Lloyd tender *Willkommen*.

He did his military service between November 1927 and May 1929 in Toulon, serving on board the carrier *Béarn* and aviso (escort ship) *Ailette*. He was a Reserve officer until 1964.

Le Roi was an international seafarer for ten years (1929–39) and made fifty voyages. The last one was to Indochina. He was a second officer and later first officer for the Compagnie des Chargeurs Réunis shipping line. He travelled to Africa, Indochina, India, Ceylan, Egypt, Maroco, Brazil, Argentine, Uruguay, Germany, and Belgium. He was affected in various ports in France (Bordeaux, Le Havre, Dunkirk, Cherbourg) and abroad (Djibouti, Singapore, Rotterdam, Antwerp, Hamburg, Dakar, Bathurst, Conakry, Monrovia, etc.). Ironically he never travelled to the United Kingdom.

Le Roi stopped sailing at sea when France and UK declared war on Germany in 1939. He instead became a port pilot until 18 June 1940. He refused to work during the German occupation. After the liberation of Cherbourg he served again as a pilot until November 1944.

Captain André Le Roi. (Collection Bernard Le Roi)

Le Roi served on various tankers on the Mediterranean Sea from 1945 to 1948 and was later hired by the Société Cherbourgeoise de Remoquage et de Sauvetage. Captain Le Roi commanded tenders *Ingénieur Minard* and *La Bretonnière* from 1948 to 1962.

His son Bernard Le Roi still remembers RMS *Queen Elizabeth* and RMS *Queen Mary* calling in Cherbourg on Mondays and Thursdays as well as United States, Norddeutscher Lloyd, Royal Mail and other Greek liners. André invited Bernard on board *Ingénieur Minard* many times. Even when giant liners were docking directly alongside the maritime station, the tender was used to ferry mailbags, freight, baggage or cars.

Le Roi left Cherbourg when he retired in 1962 and moved back to his birthplace in Regnéville-sur-Mer. He was decorated as Knight in the Order of Maritime Merit in 1964. He died on 29 April 1982.

Clockwise from left: Captain André Le Roi on *Ingénieur Minard*'s bridge in 1952. (Bernard Le Roi collection); *Ingénieur Minard* and RMS *Queen Elizabeth*. (Fonds Maurice Lucas, Archives Départementales de la Manche); *Ingénieur Minard* approaching RMS *Queen Elizabeth* in the 1950s. Note she was still flying the White Star Line flag. (Günter Bäbler collection); *Ingénieur Minard* and RMS *Queen Mary* in the 1960s. (Author's collection)

Ingénieur Minard and RMS *Queen Mary* in 1955. (Fonds Maurice Lucas, Archives Départementales de la Manche)

Ingénieur Minard seen from SS *Hanseatic*'s deck. (Fonds Maurice Lucas, Archives Départementales de la Manche)

"QUEEN ELIZABETH" ET "QUEEN MARY" — LES PLUS GRANDS NAVIRES DU MONDE

CUNARD LINE

AVRIL 1960

ARRIVÉES A CHERBOURG			DÉPARTS DE CHERBOURG		
VENANT DE NEW YORK			POUR NEW YORK		
Lundi	4 Avril	QUEEN ELIZABETH	Jeudi	7 Avril	QUEEN ELIZABETH
Lundi	11 "	QUEEN MARY	Jeudi	14 "	QUEEN MARY
Lundi	18 "	QUEEN ELIZABETH	Jeudi	21 "	QUEEN ELIZABETH
Lundi	25 "	QUEEN MARY	Jeudi	28 "	QUEEN MARY

ARRIVÉES AU HAVRE			DÉPARTS DU HAVRE		
VENANT DE NEW YORK			POUR LE CANADA		
Vendredi	8 Avril	IVERNIA	Samedi	2 Avril	SAXONIA
			Vendredi	15 "	IVERNIA
VENANT DU CANADA			Samedi	30 "	SAXONIA
Vendredi	8 Avril	IVERNIA			
Jeudi	21 "	SAXONIA			

Clockwise from left: Cunard White Star schedules, April 1960. (Author's collection); *Ingénieur Minard* greeting SS *Hanseatic*. (Fonds Maurice Lucas, Archives Départementales de la Manche); *Ingénieur Minard* approaching SS *Hanseatic*. (Fonds Maurice Lucas, Archives Départementales de la Manche); *Ingénieur Minard, Ingénieur Cachin* and Société Cherbourgeoise de Remorquage et de Sauvetage tugs in 1952. (Fonds Maurice Lucas, Archives Départementales de la Manche)

Ingénieur Minard in October 1968. (Peter Robert, Ken Marschall collection)

The first-class area in 1968. (Peter Robert, Ken Marschall collection)

Ingénieur Minard's reciprocating steam engine as seen through the engine room skylight. (Peter Robert, Ken Marschall collection)

Ingénieur Minard serving RMS *Queen Elizabeth* in July 1968. (Author's collection)

Ingénieur Minard in October 1968. (Peter Robert, Ken Marschall collection)

Nomadic in Paris in 1975. (Allen Hubbard,
Ken Marschall collection)

s/s NOMADIC

Port Debilly 75016 Paris tél. 720.67.69

A *Nomadic* advertising booklet. (Author's collection)

The Shogun restaurant on board the *Nomadic*. (Author's collection)

Le Colonial restaurant
on board the *Nomadic*.
(Author's collection)

Le Colonial restaurant on board the *Nomadic*. (Author's collection)

A *Nomadic* model used in the 1997 movie *Titanic.* (Ken Marschall, courtesy of Digital Domain)

Ken Marschall with the *Nomadic* model used in the movie
Titanic. (Photo courtesy of Parks Stephenson)

Nomadic in Paris in 1996. (Ken Marschall collection)

Set-up for a wedding on board *Nomadic* in the 1980s. (Author's collection)

Nomadic on the Seine in 1980. (Dennis Kromm, Ken Marschall collection)

Nomadic leaving Paris on 1 April 2003.
(Günter Bäbler collection)

Nomadic leaving Paris on 1 April 2003. (Günter Bäbler collection)

Nomadic being lowered onto the submersible barge on
9 July 2006. (Author's collection)

Nomadic arriving in Belfast on 15 July 2006. (John McDonald)

Steel work begins on *Nomadic* in 2011. (Mervyn Pritchard)

This page and opposite: *Nomadic* during her restoration in 2011. (Author's collection)

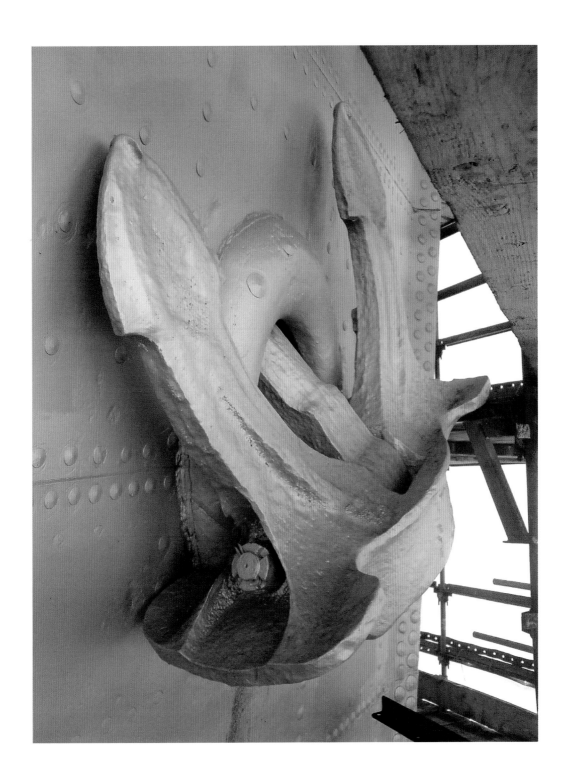

An original wooden panel of *Nomadic*'s was found in France in 2006 and transported back to Belfast. (Mervyn Pritchard)

Nomadic Preservation Society volunteers cleaning *Nomadic*'s propellers. (Mervyn Pritchard)

The grand opening of the restored *Nomadic* on 31 May 2013. (Author's collection)

Above and following pages: *Nomadic* in February 2018. (Author's collection)

No. 2 Lifeboat from *Nomadic* undergoing restoration. (*Nomadic* Preservation Society collection)

CHAPTER 9

THE END OF THE LINE

When Captain Le Roi retired in 1962 the level of transatlantic traffic had stabilised to an average of 50,000 passengers a year. But this quickly collapsed to 40,000 in 1965 and 20,000 in 1966.

Captain Longuemare took command of *Ingénieur Minard*, replacing André Le Roi on the bridge of the 51-year-old tender. He was the tenth captain to command the ship.

At that time, Société Cherbourgeoise de Remoquage et de Sauvetage tenders were very little used. They ensured 'express' service when transatlantic liners did not dock at the port or in case of bad weather. When the Cunard White Star decided to withdraw RMS *Queen Mary* and RMS *Queen Elizabeth* from service, it spelled the end of Cherbourg as a transatlantic port of call on the Southampton–New York line. *Queen Mary* said farewell to Cherbourg on 27 September 1967 and *Queen Elizabeth* called at Cherbourg for the last time on 4 November 1968. On 5 November 1968, *Ouest France* newspaper wrote:

> Symbol of a bygone era, the world's largest ocean liner bids farewell to our port. The people of Cherbourg who saw Charles Lindbergh on his way back to USA after his first non-stop transatlantic crossing in 1927 had no idea that some forty years later the plane would have definitely supplanted the boat on the intercontinental routes. One year after her sister, *Queen Elizabeth* has sounded three times the deep and moving voice of her whistle in response to the fraternal greeting of the tender *Ingénieur Minard*. No official demonstration of sympathy marked the end of these nearly fifty years of friendship between Cherbourg and Cunard. The company separates itself definitively from a port which has so well served its interests. Sadness, melancholy and very keen anxiety on the part of the people of Cherbourg who see their source of work plunge into crisis. To help the dockers forget their bitterness, the Cunarder made only a brief stop, one of her fastest, although there were 400 passengers to carry. For her last transatlantic crossing, the steamer suffered a violent storm in the North Atlantic, which explains a long delay. She entered Cherbourg waters at 6.30 p.m. Tenders *Ingénieur Minard* and *La Bretonnière* ferried 280 cross-Channel passengers, 139 travellers to Paris and some representatives of Cunard in France. The Towage and Salvage Company, whose staff is largely fired, is going to scrap its last two tenders.

The Cunard White Star closed its Cherbourg office on 7 November 1968. A few months earlier, the Towing and Salvage Company already faced forty-three redundancies.

The port of Cherbourg closed the page of transatlantic transport and *Ingénieur Minard* tender was sold to the Société Maritime Industrielle de Récupération scrapyard.

Minard, as the people of Cherbourg called her, just escaped the demolition thanks to Roland Spinnewyn, a French entrepreneur in the barge sector, who bought the steamship to turn her into a floating restaurant. On 26 April 1969, the tender formerly know as *Nomadic* was towed to Le Havre and then Rouen. Superstructures on the Flying Bridge deck that would not allow her to pass under the bridges on the Seine River were removed and the towing resumed to Conflans-Sainte-Honorine.

Ingénieur Minard and Société Cherbourgeoise de Remorquage et de Sauvetage tugs and tenders. (Fonds Maurice Lucas, Archives Départementales de la Manche)

Ingénieur Minard serving RMS *Queen Mary*. (Author's collection)

Elizabeth Taylor and Richard Burton disembarking *Ingénieur Minard* on 12 October 1964. (Jean-Marie Lezec)

Ingénieur Minard at the Quai de Normandie.
(Author's collection)

Ingénieur Minard and RMS *Queen Elizabeth*.
(Author's collection)

Ingénieur Minard at the *Quai de Normandie* in 1964. (Author's collection)

Ingénieur Minard unused in 1968. (Jean-Marie Lezec)

Ingénieur Minard in the Bassin du Commerce in 1968. (Author's collection)

RMS *Queen Elizabeth*'s last call in Cherbourg on 4 November 1968. (Fonds Maurice Lucas, Archives Départementales de la Manche)

Captain Longuemare on *Ingénieur Minard*'s bridge watching RMS *Queen Elizabeth* on her last visit to Cherbourg. (*Ouest France*, 5 November 1968, Fonds Maurice Lucas, Archives Départementales de la Manche)

10

A SECOND LIFE

Ingénieur Minard spent more than four years in Conflans. The dismantled funnel, mast, wheelhouse and Welin Quadrant davits were kept on board for some time. The ship lost her engine and boiler rooms. Metals were sold to a nearby scrap dealer.

Moored at the Quai du Confluent on the Oise River, the tender was regularly 'visited' by looters. Unfortunately, many precious metals disappeared, including the bronze bell, as well as porcelain, brass and other valuable materials.

During that time, Mr Spinnewyn was still hesitant to finalise his project. A model of the future restaurant had been created, but his plans were never realised. The ship was eventually sold to a Parisian estate agent, Yvon Vincent, and his brother.

Minard travelled up the River Seine in October 1974, ballasted with 800 tons of water to pass the bridges of Paris. Her luxurious interior fittings were adapted to her new vocation as a meeting and reception centre. The transformation works took nearly three years. By 1977, *Nomadic*, having regained her original name, is also restored to the traditional silhouette of a seagoing ship.

On 25 June 1977, Europe 1 radio channel inaugurated *Nomadic* with a vast reception on the occasion of the Paris Carnival organised by French radio columnist Pierre Bellemare.

Several restaurants alternated on board from 1977 to 1999: the Shogun Asian restaurant was followed by Le Colonial. Taking advantage of the renewed interest in *Titanic* created by James Cameron's 1998 film, the restaurant changed its name to Le Transbordeur du *Titanic* (The Tender of the *Titanic*). Various events were held in the 1,200m² available space: casino nights, dancing, fashion shows, weddings, banquets, cocktails, openings … *Nomadic* became 'the place to be' in Paris!

Almost twenty years after the start of her second life, *Nomadic*, like all the boats moored on the Seine River in Paris, became subject to new safety regulations imposing an annual dry-dock examination. Since her arrival, the ship has largely been transformed. The original superstructures had been replaced by modern facilities, ensuring more comfort for visitors, including air conditioning, spacious kitchens and large windows in the restaurant area with an impressive view of the Eiffel Tower. But due to the many changes to her superstructures, *Nomadic* was trapped between the Iena and the Debilly bridges. The mandatory examination outside Paris would require the partial dismantling of these modern elements and the suspension of *Nomadic*'s commercial activities. Administrative and financial concerns increased from late 1999. The operating licence of the restaurant was withdrawn the following year, plunging her owner into financial bankruptcy.

In France, the Ministry of Culture temporarily listed *Nomadic* on the Heritage Register for a period of one year starting on 8 April 2003, providing a buyer to carry out the historic restoration project was found. Despite some interest in Cherbourg and Monaco, no real commitment was to be found.

After years of legal procedures and Yvon Vincent's death in March 2005, the Port of Paris sought to dispose of the vessel. On learning of her fate, heritage and maritime enthusiasts mobilised to avoid her destruction. The ship has also been suffering from poor maintenance for many years and some were concerned about the ship sinking in the high-traffic river.

In Northern Ireland, the City of Belfast also shown an interested, and several enthusiasts, federated under the 'Nomadic Appeal' banner, tried to raise enough money to repatriate the ship to her birthplace and have her restored by the shipyard that built her. Lobbyists pulled up their sleeves and funds were collected from the public with the aim of buying the only White Star Line ship still existing in the world. As part of this commitment, the author Philippe Delaunoy, who had been working for the return of the *Nomadic* to Belfast since the summer of 2000, was collecting a multitude of original artefacts that could later be used for the ship's restoration.

Nomadic left Paris on 1 April 2003 and was towed again to Le Havre. The ship's condition has been evaluated and *Nomadic* was

found in a relative good shape. By the expiration of the deadline set by the French authorities, no serious project was proposed, and the Port of Paris's Legal Department eventually proceeded to her judicial sale. If no buyer appeared, *Nomadic* risked being sold for scrap value!

The first auction held in November 2005 did not find a buyer and a second hearing was scheduled for 26 January 2006. Campaigners were well supported by the public, particularly in Northern Ireland, but were unable to raise sufficient funds to meet *Nomadic*'s reserve price. The campaigns, however, gained political and governmental support, and on 26 January the Northern Irish government's Department for Social Development (DSD) bought the vessel for €250,001. It was a great victory for all those who dreamed of seeing *Titanic*'s tender back in her birthplace!

Ingénieur Minard leaving Cherbourg in April 1969. (Jean-Marie Lezec)

Above and following pages: *Ingénieur Minard* on the Oise River in Conflans-Sainte-Honorine. (Bernard Le Roi Collection)

(Archives Départementales de la Manche)

(Archives Départementales de la Manche)

Nomadic on the River Seine in Paris in 1977. (Author's collection)

Advertising for the 1977
Paris Carnival. (Author's
collection)

Ouverture

NOMADIC TRANSBORDEUR DU TITANIC

1909 White Star Line construit le TITANIC et le Nomadic
1912 Le Nomadic effectue le transbordement des passagers du TITANIC

BÂTEAU TRANSBORDEUR DU TITANIC
ENTRE LE PONT D'IENA ET LE PONT DE L'ALMA (VOIR PLAN AU DOS)
TEL. : 01 49 52 06 07

RIVE DROITE - PORT DEBILLY
à hauteur du 26 avenue de NEW-YORK - 75016 PARIS

Menu **TITANIC** *à 100 frs*

ENTREES	PLATS
6 escargots de Bourgogne	Poulet fermier rôti et son gratin
Les Moules à la marinière	La pièce de bœuf à la bordelaise
La salade au roquefort	Le filet de canard au poivre des Iles
La salade de fruits de mer	Le saumon frais à l'oseille

DESSERTS
Tarte tatin chaude
Mousse au chocolat "Maison"
Salade fruit frais etc.

Ouvert 7j/7
de 12 h à 1 h du matin   *Service Non stop*

Bâteau NOMADIC TRANSBORDEUR DU TITANIC
Port Debilly - hauteur quai 26, avenue de New York 75016 Paris

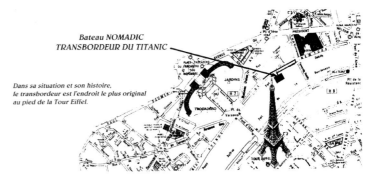

Bateau NOMADIC
TRANSBORDEUR DU TITANIC

Dans sa situation et son histoire,
le transbordeur est l'endroit le plus original
au pied de la Tour Eiffel.

Réservation clients "Hôtels" Tél. : 01 49 52 06 07

Le Transbordeur du *Titanic* restaurant. (Author's collection)

Nomadic celebrates the fiftieth anniversary of the 1931 Citroën expedition to Asia. (Author's collection)

Nomadic on the Seine in April 1996. (Ken Marschall collection)

Nomadic's Welin Quadrant davits stored on the Quai Debilly in 1980. (Dennis Kromm, Ken Marschall collection)

Nomadic's No. 1 Lifeboat stored on the Quai Debilly in 1980. (Dennis Kromm, Ken Marschall collection)

Nomadic on the Seine in 1980. (Dennis Kromm, Ken Marschall collection)

Nomadic on the Seine in 1980. (Dennis Kromm, Ken Marschall collection)

Nomadic leaving Paris on 1 April 2003. (Günter Bäbler collection)

Above and right: *Nomadic* in Le Havre in 2004. (Author's collection)

Above and following pages: *Nomadic* being lowered on the submersible barge on 9 July 2006. (Author's collection)

11

BACK TO BELFAST

Following the acquisition of the vessel in January 2006, the DSD created the body that would run the ship's restoration project, the *Nomadic* Charitable Trust (NCT). The '*Nomadic* Appeal' brought itself into the *Nomadic* Preservation Society, sitting on NCT with representatives of DSD, the Port of Belfast, the Belfast City Council and other heritage societies.

Nomadic stayed in Le Havre for some months and preliminary works were done in order to prepare her return to Belfast. The ship was loaded on to a submersible barge on 9 July 2006 and towed to Belfast through the Channel and the Irish Sea. The convoy reached Belfast Harbour on 15 July.

Still well secured on her barge, *Nomadic* was presented to the public for a few days. English and Irish media rushed to immortalise the moment. However, a slight detail seemed to have been forgotten …

Having spent a little more than three years in Le Havre, the ship's hull was colonised by algae and shells. Isolated from her aquatic element for several days, the organic decomposition gave off an unpleasant smell under the hot weather that prevailed in Belfast in the summer of 2006. It would be unfortunate if official speeches, enhanced by the presence of Minister Hanson, were 'embellished' with the aroma of decaying molluscs, so Harland & Wolff shipyard workers were put to work and, armed with powerful high-pressure cleaners, they eliminated the majority of parasites. But in the heatwave, the strenuous work resulted in one of the shipyard workers contracting heatstroke, from which he died. As a result, the festivities planned were reduced to a minimum in tribute to the victim.

The following months were used to carry out various studies on the vessel and to develop the Conservation Management Plan. *Nomadic* was first opened to the public in April 2007. Volunteers from the *Nomadic* Preservation Society set up a temporary exhibition and did the necessary work to accommodate visitors. 18,000 people flocked to appreciate this precious witness of local know-how in shipbuilding.

The heavy reconstruction work was split into two phases: the 'steel' works and the 'fitting out'. The renovation project needed a place specifically dedicated to this purpose. The Hamilton dry dock, where *Nomadic*'s fitting out took place in 1911, seemed to be quite appropriate. The dock was also completely restored, allowing the site to function optimally and, in the long run, will provide a historic setting for *Nomadic* as a tourist attraction.

STEEL WORKS

This important and spectacular aspect of the project was not only dedicated to rebuilding the missing elements of the ship – the bridge deck, flying bridge deck, funnel and gangways, amongst other things – but also to ensure a perfect seal to protect the hull against corrosion.

In addition, since the project was financed in part by the Lottery Heritage Fund, the historical aspect of the vessel had to be maintained. Craft techniques were used to recreate superstructures, railing, stairs and vents. It would be inconceivable to use welders when the steel was originally riveted.

NO. 2 LIFEBOAT

Following their removal from the vessel in 1969, *Nomadic*'s two lifeboats were placed in an outside courtyard at the former Chantereyne museum in Cherbourg, where they received little attention for over twenty-five years.

Only the No. 2 Lifeboat survived, though in a poor condition, and it was identified by the *Nomadic* Preservation Society's European coordinator, Philippe Delaunoy, and acquired by them in 2007. It has also been returned to Belfast for restoration.

The only surviving lifeboat from the White Star Line tender *Nomadic*, which is known to have been carried on Welin Quadrant davits on the starboard side of the Flying Bridge Deck, is a rare survivor of the more traditional type of clinker-built lifeboat, of planks of wood overlapping downwards and secured by copper rivets. Slightly smaller, it is similar in style and construction to the two cutters carried on RMS *Titanic*.

It was designed by Roderick Chisholm, chief draughtsman of Harland & Wolff, and built in the boatbuilders' shed at the company's shipyard. It appears to survive in its original form though it was surveyed in May 2009 and found to be in a very bad state of repair.

SS *Nomadic*'s No. 2 Lifeboat is exceptional in many aspects: she was built by one of the most important shipbuilding companies in the world, and she was used on a vessel which served many of the world's great ocean liners, including the *Olympic*-class vessels of the White Star Line, in particular the ill-fated *Titanic*. There is evidence that *Nomadic* lifeboats were employed many times during the First World War for minesweeping activities. No. 2 Lifeboat is known to have saved lives in 1928 and 1936 when sailors fell into Cherbourg Harbour's waters.

No. 2 Lifeboat is one of only four preserved ship lifeboats included on the National Small Boat Register (Registration No. 1616). She is therefore of considerable historical and cultural importance as a rare, and possibly unique, survivor of a *Titanic*-era lifeboat and the only one in the world preserved from the White Star Line.

Nomadic's No. 2 Lifeboat stored at the Musée Chantereyne in Cherbourg. (Musée Chantereyne)

Technical data:
Length: 19ft 6in
Beam: 5ft 6in
Deep: 2ft 3in
Approximate capacity:
twenty-eight people

No. 2 Lifeboat restored and on
display in April 2016. (Author's
collection)

Nomadic's No. 2 Lifeboat in 1911.
(Günter Bäbler collection)

Once these imposing elements were installed, a new teak deck was placed and the caulking carried out. *Nomadic* was then perfectly sealed against infiltration of rainwater and work could begin inside the ship.

FITTING OUT

The interior of the ship had been transformed many times during her stay in Paris, and so considerable work was undertaken to not only reinstall original items on board but also to produce copies for missing panels, replace destroyed elements, recreate the spaces and the saloons according to the original plan, and install electricity, lighting, plumbing and sanitary facilities.

The 1910 Harland & Wolff General Arrangement Plan clearly mentioned the use of linoleum. This coating composed of burlap, linseed oil and wood powder (or cork) had excellent resistance to wear and allowed easy cleaning. A fragment of the original linoleum was discovered on the site of the former first-class toilets aboard *Nomadic*. The design, well known to *Titanic* historians, allowed immediate identification and a single production was commissioned, so that *Nomadic* could regain her original appearance from floor to ceiling.

Although some elements had yet to be completed – including masts, davits, lifeboats and the covered wheelhouse – the inauguration of *Nomadic* as a first-class tourist attraction took place on 31 May 2013. This date was chosen to coincide with the anniversary of the launch of *Titanic* on 31 May 1911.

Presented to visitors in the Hamilton Dry Dock, *Nomadic* will unfortunately never sail again. At over 100 years old, the tender has miraculously escaped destruction on many occasions. She has benefited from a truly prodigious chance, since today she is definitively saved and preserved for future generations to enjoy and discover.

ACKNOWLEDGEMENTS

This book is the result of eighteen years of research and the brainchild of many conversations between transatlantic liners enthusiasts all around the world.

I have to start by thanking my awesome wife, Sandrine. From helping me analysing hundreds of archive documents to giving advice on the selection of pictures, she was an important supporter. Thank you so much, dear!

Amy Rigg is the very first person I met in the publishing industry. She provided a lot of valuable advices and guided me during the long elaboration process of such a project.

Renowned historians and researchers kindly agreed to collaborate by providing useful pictures and sharing stories. Ken Marschall, Günther Babler and Jean Pivain are some of them. The quality of the documents they provided is just wonderful. Thank you, guys!

I had the privilege to meet various *Nomadic* crew members' families. I would like to express my deepest gratitude to them for sharing their own stories and family archives. They all contributed greatly to perfect our knowledge about the ship's history. I wish to thank Annie and Philippe Duval, Alain Cozic, Bernard Ade, Bernard Le Roi, Marcelle Leplanquet, Béatrice Holzbacher as well as Les Archives Départementales de la Manche, the Service Historique de la Défense in Cherbourg, the Imperial War Museum, Kerrie Sweeney and the *Titanic* Belfast Foundation, and National Museums NI and the Harland & Wolff Collection (Ulster Folk & Transport Museum).

The continuous interest from *Nomadic* and *Titanic* enthusiasts all over the world provided me the essential inspiration for writing this book. I would like to express my gratitude to Mervyn Pritchard, Darryl Leblanc, Jerry Vondeling, Cyril and Lionel Codus, Olivier Mendez, Andrei Louis Alejandro, Parks Stephenson and John McDonald for their help and investment.

Individually, I would like to give thanks for support to: Commodore Ronald W. Warwick OBE, David Scott Beddard, the British Titanic Society, the Deutscher Titanic Verein, the Titanic Verein Schweiz, the Association Française du Titanic, Pierre Bellemare and Digital Domain.

APPENDIX 1

SS NOMADIC/INGENIEUR MINARD CREW LISTS 1911-40

23 May 1911–31 July 1911: Belfast–Cherbourg Voyage

CAPTAIN

Pierre François Bouétard

(disembark 31 August 1911)

SECOND OFFICER

Joseph Ropers

CHIEF ENGINEER

Maurice Fillon (1875–1958)

SECOND ENGINEER

Henri Thomas

SEAMEN

Georges Esnol; Séraphin Glajean; François Kerambrun; Henri Duval; Gustave Durand; Pierre-Marie Caudal

STOKERS

Charles Constant, (alias Dusseaux); Pierre Grouet ; Herlé Le Corre (disembark 9 July 1911); Clément Rouspard (disembark 5 June1911); Jérôme Bréard (disembark 3 June 1911); François Bignon (disembark 3 June 1911); Lucien Delamer (embark 5 July 1911), Alfred Marais

WAITER

Auguste Ade

APPRENTICES

Emile Doairé, Yves Marie André

1 August 1911–1 July 1912*

CAPTAIN
Pierre François Bouétard (disembark 31 August 1911); **Charles Patris** (from 1 September 1911)
SECOND OFFICER
Joseph Ropers
CHIEF ENGINEER
Maurice Fillon
SECOND ENGINEER
Henri Thomas (disembark 9 September 1911); **Louis Marion** (embark 3 January 1912)
SEAMEN
Georges Esnol, Séraphin Glajean (disembark 5 June 1912), **François Kerambrun, Henri Duval, Pierre Marie Candal** (disembark 8 May 1912), **Jean-Louis Cozic,** (disembark 17 May 1912), **François Longuemare, Gustave Durand** (disembark 18 May 1912), **Paul Postel** (embark 2 January 1912 – became waiter in 1919), Louis Leledier (embark 9 May 1912), Edouard Corbin (embark 9 June 1912)
WAITER
Auguste Ade
STOKERS
Lucien Delamer (disembark 29 August 1911), **Alfred, alias Ernest, Marais, Edouard Costa, Celestin Ade** (disembark 6 September 1912), **Jules Leprince, Lucien Corre** (embark 22 September 1911)
APPRENTICE
Yves André (disembark 01 October 1911), **Eugène Cozic** (disembark 17 May 1912), Robert Leven (embark 5 June 1912), Victor Béquet (embark 22 July 1912)
* *names in **bold** are those who served RMS* Titanic *on 10 April 1912*

1 June 1919–31 December 1929

CAPTAIN
Jean Le Briand (from 1 June 1919 to 18 December 1929); Elie Gauthier (embark 29 December 1929)
SECOND OFFICER
Jean-François Le Lauz (from 4 March 1921 to 31 May 1923); Leprince Beinaimé (from 1 June 1923 to 31 May 1928); Louis Bertheaume (from 1 June 1927)
CHIEF ENGINEER
Maurice Fillon

SECOND ENGINEER

Louis Marion (disembark 19 October 1919); Auguste Esterlingot (from 1 June to 3 July 1920); Georges Rodeiron (from 4 July 1920 to 3 January 1921); Louis Marion (from 4 January 1921 to 31 May 1927); Jean Marèvre (from 1 June 1927 to 18 December 1929; Albert Mesnage (embark 19 December 1929)

ENGINEERING ASSISTANT

Lucien Carre

SEAMEN

Eugène Dessoux; Alexandre Ganneville; Pierre Ropers (embark 1 September 1919); Jean Trechrieu; Charles Le Blond (embark 1 September 1919); Fernand Auvray, Joseph Auvray (from 8 July 1919 to 5 February 1920); Georges Esnol (from 6 September 1919 to 13 August 1923); Georges Bequet (embark 11 September 1919); Jean Baptiste Leprince (from 1 June 1920 to 21 October 1924); Joseph Valognes (embark 1 June 1920); Bouin Louis (embark 1 June 1923); Victor Laé (embark 1 June 1923); Charles Bellot (embark 22 October 1924); Ferdinand Riou (from 3 November 1924 to 20 March 1925); Jean Lecourt (embark 6 February 1925); Constant Léonard (embark 21 March 1925); Pierre Ropus (embark 1 June 1925); Charles Bertheaume (embark 1 October 1926); Jean Delaporte (from 1 June 1928, previously apprentice); Emmanuel Leraux (embark 1 June 1927); Emile Ricard (embark 1 December 1929)

FIRST STOKER

Jean Hamelin (embark 1 June 1929)

SIGNALMAN

Carr Thomas (UK citizen)

STOKERS

Eugène Renouf; Théodore Le Doaré (embark 1 September 1919); François Troadec (disembark 19 June 1919); Pierre Thomas (embark 28 June 1919); Charles Le Glac (embark 30 June 1919); Nicolas Le Guillau (from 8 July to 21 August 1919); Nicolas Lelong (embark 9 July 1919); Jules Leprince (embark 22 August 1919); François Piroivin (from 22 August 1919 to 1 May 1920); Marie Roidat (embark 25 August 1919); Henri Coupey (embark 9 September 1919); Emile Pivain (disembark 31 May 1921); Jean Dupont (from 1 June 1920 to 29 January 1921; Octave Brotin (embark 1 February 1921), Jean Alexandre (embark 1 June 1923), Désiré Heudon (embark 21 November 1924)

CARPENTER

Adolphe Coligneaux (embark 14 August 1920)

COOK

Victor Laé (embark 1 September 1919)

WAITER

Paul Postel (from 1 September 1919)

APPRENTICES

Alfred Dessoux (disembark 10 June 1919), Léon Lesage (embark 1 September 1919), Robert Puel (from 21 January 1921 to 31 April 1924), Paul Léonard (from 24 September 1924 to 31 May 1928), Jean Delaporte (from 01 June 1926 to 27 february 1927), Aurélier Lemaitre (embark 9 october 1926), Gabriel Lelouey (embark 01/06/1928)

1 June 1930–31 March 1934

CAPTAIN

Elie Gauthier (disembark 1 June 1932); Auguste Roulet (from 1 June 1932 to 30 September 1933);
Léopold Rabecq (embark 1 October 1933)

SECOND OFFICER

Louis Bertheaume (disembark 30 May 1932); Louis Duédal (embark 1 June 1932)

CHIEF ENGINEER

Louis Marion

SECOND ENGINEER

Albert Mesnage (disembark 30 September 1933; ran a wireless shop in Cherbourg); Jean Rolland
(embark 1 October 1933)

SEAMEN

Georges Bequet (from 1 June 1930 to 2 January 1934); Joseph Valognes; Victor Laé; Charles Bellot; Jean
Lecourt; Pierre Ropers; Constant Léonard; Jean Delaporte; Emile Ricard (disembark 31 March 1933);
Auguste Tournel (embark 1 June 1932); Auguste Durand (embark 1 June 1932); Louis Leledier (embark
1 June 1932); Yves Le Berre (embark 1 June 1932); Edouard Leterrier (from 1 to 31 March 1933);
Theophile Fatin (embark 1 June 1933), Joseph Le Bas (from 1 June to 3 June 1933), Ernest Leledier (from
1 April 1937 to 15 December 1938); Henri Ansot (embark 1 April 1937); Michel Leparmentier (embark
27 January 1938); Eugène Laurent (embark 1 April 1939); Gustave Croisier (embark 1 April 1939); Louis
Le Rolland (embark 1 April 1939)

SIGNALMAN

Thomas Carr

CARPENTER

Auguste Fournel; Pierre Griesseman; Adolphe Coligneaux (embark 01 April 1939)

STOKERS

Jean Hamelin; Thédore Le Doaré; Henri Coupey; Désiré Heudon; Albert Vasquez (embark 01/06/1932);
Ange Millot (embark 1 June 1932); Auguste Hacquez (embark 1 June 1933);
Pierre Mourfiel (embark 1 April 1939); Alcinne Burmel (embark 1 April 1939)

APPRENTICES

Gabriel Lelouey (from 1 June 1932 to 30 May 1933); Gabriel Lelouez (embark 1 June 1933); René
Leledier (embark 1 April 1934); Yves Tallegas (embark 1 April 1934); F. Thoraval (embark 1 April 1938);
Ferdinand Fichet (embark 1 April 1939); Edouard Aunay (embark 1 April 1939)

Post-Second World War Captains

Léopold Rabecq: 1945–48
André Le Roi: 1948–62
Captain Longuemare: 1962–68

APPENDIX 2

RMS TITANIC CROSS-CHANNEL PASSENGERS

(SOUTHAMPTON–CHERBOURG)

First- and second-class passengers disembarking in Cherbourg on 10 April 1912:

BRAND	Mr	1st Class	LENOX-CONYNGHAM	Mr Dennis	1st Class
COLLIS	Mr	1st Class	LENOX-CONYNGHAM	Mrs Barbara	1st Class
DAVIES	Miss K.	2nd Class	LENOX-CONYNGHAM	Miss Harriet	1st Class
DAVIES	Mr H.V.	2nd Class	LENOX-CONYNGHAM	Miss Eileen	1st Class
DE GRASSE	Mr J.	2nd Class	MULLEN		2nd Class
DYER EDWARDES	Mrs Clementina	1st Class	REMESCH	Miss	2nd Class
DYER EDWARDES	Mr Thomas	1st Class	STEVENS	Mr George	1st Class
EVANS	Miss	2nd Class	TOVEY	Miss	2nd Class
FLETCHER	Miss	1st Class	WOTTON	Mr Henry	1st Class
FORMAN	Mrs	1st Class	NOEL	Mr William	1st Class
FORMAN	Mr	1st Class	NOEL	Major Gerard	1st Class
KNEESE	Miss	2nd Class	OSBORNE	Miss	2nd Class

APPENDIX 3

SS NOMADIC FIRST- AND SECOND-CLASS PASSENGERS

Passengers ferried by *Nomadic* to RMS *Titanic* on 10 April 1912:

Surname	First Names	Survivor (S) or Victim (V)	Class
Andrews	Miss Kornelia Theodosia	S	First Class
Artagaveytia	Mr Ramon	V	First Class
Astor	Colonel John Jacob	V	First Class
Astor	Mrs Madeleine Talmage	S	First Class
Aubart	Mme. Léontine Pauline	S	First Class
Bassani	Mrs Albina	S	First Class
Baumann	Mr John D.	V	First Class
Baxter	Mrs Hélène	S	First Class
Baxter	Mr Quigg Edmond	V	First Class
Behr	Mr Karl Howell	S	First Class
Bertoccini			First Class
Bessette	Miss Nellie Mayo	S	First Class
Bidois	Miss Rosalie	S	First Class
Birnbaum	Mr Jakob	V	First Class
Bishop	Mr Dickinson H.	S	First Class

Bishop	Mrs Helen	S	First Class
Blank	Mr Henry	S	First Class
Bowen	Miss Grace Scott	S	First Class
Brandeis	Mr Emil Franklin	V	First Class
Brewe	Dr Arthur Jackson	V	First Class
Brown	Mrs Margaret	S	First Class
Bucknell	Mrs Emma Eliza	S	First Class
Burns	Miss Elizabeth Margaret	S	First Class
Candee	Mrs Helen Churchill	S	First Class
Cardeza	Mrs Charlotte Wardle	S	First Class
Cardeza	Mr Thomas Drake Martinez	S	First Class
Cassebeer	Mrs Eleanor Genevieve	S	First Class
Chaudanson	Miss Victorine	S	First Class
Chevré	Mr Paul Romaine Marie Léonce	S	First Class
Clark	Mr Walter Miller	V	First Class
Clark	Mrs Virginia Estelle	S	First Class
Compton	Mrs Mary Eliza	S	First Class
Compton	Miss Sara Rebecca	S	First Class
Compton	Mr Alexander Taylor Jr	V	First Class
Cumings	Mr John Bradley	V	First Class
Cumings	Mrs Florence Briggs	S	First Class
Davidson	Mr Thornton	V	First Class
Davidson	Mrs Orian	S	First Class
Douglas	Mr Walter Donald	V	First Class
Douglas	Mrs Mahala	S	First Class
Douglas	Mrs Mary Hélène	S	First Class
Duff Gordon	Sir Cosmo Edmund	S	First Class
Duff Gordon	Lady Lucy Christiana	S	First Class
Dulles	Mr William Crothers	V	First Class
Earnshaw	Mrs Olive	S	First Class
Endres	Miss Caroline Louise	S	First Class
Eustis	Miss Elizabeth Mussey	S	First Class
Evans	Miss Edith Corse	V	First Class
Flegenheim	Mrs Antoinette	S	First Class
Fleming	Miss Margaret	S	First Class
Foreman	Mr Benjamin Laventall	V	First Class
Francatelli	Miss Laura Mabel	S	First Class
Frauenthal	Mr Isaac Gerald	S	First Class
Frölicher	Miss Hedwig Margaritha	S	First Class
Frölicher-Stehli	Mr Maximilian Josef	S	First Class

Frölicher-Stehli	Mrs Margaretha Emerentia	S	First Class
Gibson	Mrs Pauline Caroline	S	First Class
Gibson	Miss Dorothy Winifred	S	First Class
Giglio	Mr Victor Gaitan Andrea	V	First Class
Goldenberg	Mr Samuel L.	S	First Class
Goldenberg	Mrs Nella	S	First Class
Goldschmidt	Mr George B.	V	First Class
Greenfield	Mrs Blanche	S	First Class
Greenfield	Mr William Bertram	S	First Class
Guggenheim	Mr Benjamin	V	First Class
Harder	Mr George Achilles	S	First Class
Harder	Mrs Dorothy	S	First Class
Harper	Mr Henry Sleeper	S	First Class
Harper	Mrs Myra Raymond	S	First Class
Hassab	Mr Hammad	S	First Class
Hays	Miss Margaret Bechstein	S	First Class
Hippach	Mrs Ida Sophia	S	First Class
Hippach	Miss Jean Gertrude	S	First Class
Hogeboom	Mrs Anna Louisa	S	First Class
Hoyt	Mr William Fisher	S	First Class
Isham	Miss Ann Elizabeth	V	First Class
Kent	Mr Edward Austin	V	First Class
Leroy	Miss Berthe	S	First Class
Lesueur	Mr Gustave	S	First Class
Lewy	Mr Ervin G.	V	First Class
Lindström	Mrs Sigrid	S	First Class
Lines	Mrs Elizabeth Lindsey	S	First Class
Lines	Miss Mary Conover	S	First Class
Longley	Miss Gretchen Fiske	S	First Class
Lurette	Miss Eugénie Elise	S	First Class
Maréchal	Mr Pierre	S	First Class
Mayné	Mlle Berthe Antonine	S	First Class
Meyer	Mr Edgar Joseph	V	First Class
Meyer	Mrs Leila	S	First Class
Millet	Mr Francis Davis	V	First Class
Mock	Mr Philipp Edmund	S	First Class
Natsch	Mr Charles	V	First Class
Newell	Mr Arthur Webster	V	First Class
Newell	Miss Marjorie Anne	S	First Class
Newell	Miss Madeleine	S	First Class

Nourney	Mr Alfred	S	First Class
Oliva Y Ocana	Doña Fermina	S	First Class
Omont	Mr Alfred Fernand	S	First Class
Oviés Y Rodríguez	Mr Servando José Florentino	V	First Class
Peñasco Y Castellana	Mr Victor	V	First Class
Peñasco Y Castellana	Mrs Maria Josefa Perezde Soto y Vallejo	S	First Class
Potter	Mrs Lily Alexenia	S	First Class
Reuchlin	Mr Jonkheer Johan George	V	First Class
Rheims	Mr George Alexander Lucien	S	First Class
Righini	Mr Sante	V	First Class
Robins	Mr Victor	V	First Class
Rosenbaum	Miss Edith Louise	S	First Class
Rosenshine	Mr George	V	First Class
Rothschild	Mr Martin	V	First Class
Rothschild	Mrs Elizabeth Jane Anne	S	First Class
Ryerson	Mr Arthur Larned	V	First Class
Ryerson	Mrs Emily Maria	S	First Class
Ryerson	Miss Emily Borie	S	First Class
Ryerson	Miss Susan Parker	S	First Class
Ryerson	Master John Borie	S	First Class
Sägesser	Mlle Emma	S	First Class
Schabert	Mrs Emma	S	First Class
Silvey	Mr William Baird	V	First Class
Silvey	Mrs Alice Gray	S	First Class
Smith	Mr James Clinch	V	First Class
Smith	Mr Lucian Philip	V	First Class
Smith	Mrs Mary Eloise	S	First Class
Spedden	Mr Frederic Oakley	S	First Class
Spedden	Mrs Margaretta Corning	S	First Class
Spedden	Master Robert Douglas	S	First Class
Spencer	Mr William Augustus	V	First Class
Spencer	Mrs Marie Eugenie	S	First Class
Stengel	Mr Charles Emil Henry	S	First Class
Stengel	Mrs Annie May	S	First Class
Stephenson	Mrs Martha	S	First Class
Stewart	Mr Albert Ankeny	V	First Class
Thayer	Mr John Borland	V	First Class
Thayer	Mrs Marian Longstreth	S	First Class
Thayer	Mr John Borland Jr	S	First Class
Thorne	Miss Gertrude Maybelle	S	First Class

Tucker	Mr Gilbert Milligan Jr	S	First Class
Uruchurtu	Don. Manuel Ramirez	V	First Class
Ward	Miss Annie Moore	S	First Class
Warren	Mr Frank Manley	V	First Class
Warren	Mrs Anna Sophia	S	First Class
White	Mrs Ella	S	First Class
Williams	Mr Charles Duane	V	First Class
Williams	Mr Richard Norris II	S	First Class
Wilson	Miss Helen Alice	S	First Class
Young	Miss Marie Grice	S	First Class
Abelson	Mr Samuel	V	Second Class
Abelson	Mrs Hannah	S	Second Class
Del Carlo	Mr Sebastiano	V	Second Class
Del Carlo	Mrs Argene	S	Second Class
Durán I Moné	Señora Florentina	S	Second Class
Durán I Moné	Señora Asuncion	S	Second Class
Jerwan	Mrs Marie Marthe	S	Second Class
Laroche	Mr Joseph Philippe Lemercier	V	Second Class
Laroche	Mrs Juliette Marie Louise	S	Second Class
Laroche	Miss Simonne Marie Anne Andrée	S	Second Class
Laroche	Miss Louise	S	Second Class
Lehmann	Miss Bertha	S	Second Class
Malachard	Mr Jean-Noël	V	Second Class
Mallet	Mr Albert Denis Pierre	V	Second Class
Mallet	Mrs Antonine Marie	S	Second Class
Mallet	Master André Clement	S	Second Class
Mangiavacchi	Mr Serafino Emilio	V	Second Class
Nasser	Mr Nicholas	V	Second Class
Nasser	Mrs Adele	V	Second Class
Padron Manent	Mr Julian	S	Second Class
Pallàs I Castelló	Señor Emili	S	Second Class
Pernot	Mr René	V	Second Class
Portaluppi	Mr Emilio Ilario Giuseppe	S	Second Class
Pulbaum	Mr Franz	V	Second Class
Richard	Mr Emile Phillippe	V	Second Class
Stanton	Mr Samuel Ward	V	Second Class

THE
UNSEEN
OLYMPIC
THE SHIP IN RARE ILLUSTRATIONS

PATRICK MYLON

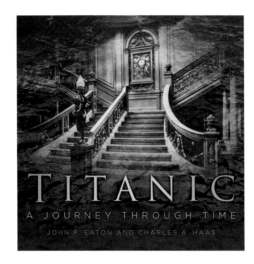

TITANIC
A JOURNEY THROUGH TIME

JOHN P. EATON AND CHARLES A. HAAS

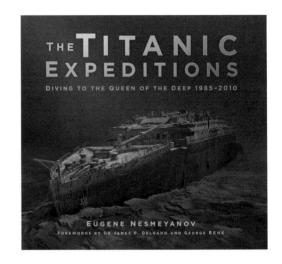

THE TITANIC
EXPEDITIONS
DIVING TO THE QUEEN OF THE DEEP 1985–2010

EUGENE NESMEYANOV
FOREWORDS BY DR JAMES P. DELGADO AND GEORGE BEHE

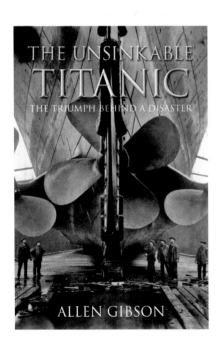

THE UNSINKABLE
TITANIC
THE TRIUMPH BEHIND A DISASTER

ALLEN GIBSON

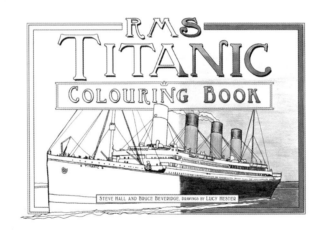

RMS
TITANIC
COLOURING BOOK

STEVE HALL AND BRUCE BEVERIDGE, DRAWINGS BY LUCY HESTER

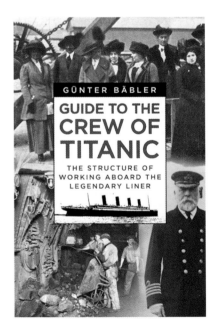

GÜNTER BÄBLER
GUIDE TO THE
CREW OF
TITANIC
THE STRUCTURE OF
WORKING ABOARD THE
LEGENDARY LINER

The History Press

The destination for history
www.thehistorypress.co.uk